Confrontation
and Learned Societies

Confrontation
and Learned Societies

Edited and with an Introduction by

JOHN VOSS
PAUL L. WARD

NEW YORK: *New York University Press*

1970

PREFACE

THE TURMOIL ON the campus, which has been a major preoccupation of students, faculty, and administrators for the last few years, is not a wholly unexpected turn of events. Seymour Martin Lipset, in a forthcoming volume analyzing the sources of student activism in America, suggests that a quiescent student population, an orderly campus, has been the exception rather than the rule in American history. Far more surprising to members of the academic professions is the fact that their professional and learned societies have also fallen under seige; in fact, the activities of one society, that of African Studies, have been brought almost to a standstill. The problems faced by these societies are less acute than those besetting university administrators—their buildings have not been burned and their computers are unscathed—but since the annual meeting of the Modern Language Association in December, 1968, no wise executive secretary of a learned society remains uninformed on strategy and tactics in dealing with confrontation.

The dissidents and activists have challenged many of the most sacred traditions of the scholarly community: value-free research and inquiry, the political neutrality of science and scholarship, and the pursuit of knowledge as an end in itself. Moreover, the *enragées* among the dissidents have denied the standard of civility and even rational discourse in relationships among scholars. Although much of this can be dismissed as a passing aberration, or in the case of the *enragées* as play-acting (what Raymond Aron has elsewhere called the psycho-drama of revolution) it raises fundamental questions about the role of scholarship and science in a society like ours which is in a state of transition or perhaps even crisis.

In order to examine critically some of these questions, the executive secretaries of the constituent organizations of the American Council of Learned Societies devoted their annual spring conference in 1969 to the theme of "Confrontation." All but one of the papers in this volume were presented at that meeting; the article by Christopher

Lasch was written later and gives his reaction to the issues raised at the symposium.

The contributors to this volume have focused on two distinct, yet interrelated, themes. The first concerns the nature and purpose of education in American society, the second the possibility that education and scholarship coexist uneasily with applied research and service in the university. Throughout these papers, there is a plea for a new synthesis of knowledge about man and society: a search for truth, not as an end in itself but in the service of man, and a process of education which emphasizes the deepest values of our society. Professor Bouwsma argues for an undergraduate education not simply as learning but as *paideia*, "the transmission of the deepest insights, attitudes, and values of a society, the most precious legacy it can pass on to succeeding generations." He recognizes, of course, that the search for *paideia* may be difficult in a pluralistic society—our society should be characterized by a number of *paideiai*—and that it may lead to "indoctrination and myth-making, an imposed conformity of mind, ethnic and cultural self-centeredness." From the perspective of the new left, Christopher Lasch voices much the same concept, if one disregards the neo-Marxist overtones, when he calls for "an integrated science of man on premises explicitly critical of industrial society," or at least of an industrial society organized by capitalism, which will "search for an interdisciplinary synthesis of critical knowledge that exists almost buried under the mountain of empirical trivia in all the disciplines relating to the study of man." On another level, Professor de Bary in an articulate defense of Western scholarship from the charge of being culture-bound maintains that Western society has isolated itself by its very success and that, until recently, we have never "had to question whether our values [rather than our scholarship] were universal." Our confrontation with non-Western cultures and with our own failures suggests the need for a new search for cultural identity through an education based on a "new world culture and humanitarianism."

Although Lasch's concept of a "science of man" is radically different from Bouwsma's pluralistic *paideiai* or de Bary's search for cultural identity, these writers share the belief that scholarship must be concerned with the big questions—truth, value, and culture in addition to learning, research and public service. They believe that these are urgent issues; and it can be argued that, in some degree, the confrontation on the campus is the result of the academic community's failure to deal with them. Yet it is possible that if the universities had developed a new *paideia* or a new science of man, the under-graduates would now be even more rebellious: in many respects youth is challenging authority itself rather than any specific kind of kind of authority.

On the other hand, as Arthur Sutherland argues so eloquently, there is no reason to bring down the house because the academic community does not provide instant truth or utopia, or because professors do not march

off in response to today's vision of the Apocalypse. Our
deepest values, he reminds us, may not be expressed in
answers to the big questions but rather in our tolerance,
our ability to question our own first principles, and,
above all, our respect for civility.

Indeed, our current problems may result not so much
from a lack of values in the academic community but
from a genuine conflict of rights in society. These rights,
and the values that rationalize these rights, are asserted
by groups at the center and periphery of society which
have been created, or at least made visible, by an affluent,
tolerant industrial society. In this situation, as Daniel Bell
has pointed out, the issue is not the conflict between
right and wrong but between right and right. If this is
true, the solution of these problems lies not so much in
the search for truth as in the process of negotiation,
compromise, and adjustment. In this process we are
likely to emerge with smaller truths and a more secure
sense of our identity.

But as we grapple with these problems, whether we
see them as big ones or as a series of smaller ones, Professor Stone reminds us that we must not undervalue
the products of scholarship—the professional base from
which the academic community operates. His paper is a
temperate reply to an intemperate attack on the MLA.
The function of a learned society is not to organize a
march against whatever social ills may be at hand, nor
even to supply answers to the big questions, but, as
Stone asserts, to discover, preserve, and disseminate what-

ever knowledge it takes for its province. Unless it maintains this flow of knowledge, discussion of values or
education will be so much empty or partisan rhetoric.

It is one thing to design a process of education
rooted in the basic values of society. It is quite another
to establish that process within the structure of the contemporary American university. Among the contributors
to this volume, there is the feeling that our universities—
overburdened with so many critical functions, immersed
in so much applied science and research, and positioned
so close to the barricades—may no longer be hospitable
to scholarship, pure research, and the search for truth
(with a big or little T).

Professor Winston suggests that universities should
"divest themselves of enterprises not directly related to
their academic purpose. One change would be a radical
redefinition of the university's role in American society.
It would involve narrowing the range of university activities, mainly by elimination of the ties to government,
industry and agriculture. By dropping their role as
'knowledge conglomerates' universities will be better
able to serve one of the primary needs of a democratic
society: freedom of inquiry and exchange." Winston further suggests a distinction between knowledge workers
and scholars; the former would deal with the application
of knowledge in special institutes, while the latter, concerned with extending the boundaries of basic knowledge, would hold academic appointments.

Winston proposes that the multi-versity be split

into its component parts. In a similar vein, Sutherland, Bouwsma, de Bary and Lasch suggest that the learned societies may play a more active role in the academic community: many of the functions of pure scholarship and interdisciplinary research would be assumed by these societies.

A strong argument can be made against the idea of a multiversity—that is, a university that encompasses education, research and service. As an educational institution, the multiversity controls access to power and status; in terms of its research functions, it is responsible for the discovery of innovative ideas and concepts in technology and the social sciences; as a service organization, it is dedicated to the application of these ideas to immediate and long-run social goals. However, in the last several years, we have discovered that the university is simply too exposed to criticism and attack from its various constituencies to carry out all of these functions at the same time. Since it is clear that the functions of education, research and service are central ones in our society and have to be maintained in some form, it is relatively easy to suggest that these functions be assigned to separate institutions, and undoubtedly some such decentralization will take place.

But the idea that scholars ought to confine themselves to the search for the Holy Grail is too easy an answer—a verbal rather than a real way out of our contemporary dilemmas. In the long run, the argument that education, research and service should be separated is not persuasive. The pure search for truth is not un-related to a choice of social priorities, whether overtly stated or intuited. In the last century, as the historian of science, Everett Mendelsohn, reminds me, the strategy of science and learning has been closely allied with a perception of such priorities. The pursuit of truth in itself is an abstraction which gives no clues as to whether resources should be devoted to molecular biol-ogy, solid state physics, medieval Latin, paleolithic ar-chaeology, or Outer Mongolian studies. In the immediate past these priorities have been set in a kind of piecemeal way by a series of dialogues or confrontations between pure and applied scientists, between scholars and funding agents. Without this dialogue, indeed this adversary proc-ess, I suspect that scholarship and pure research would become isolated and pedantic, a refuge from the real world. Much of the current frustration of the humanist arises from his frequent engagement in pure research which has no conceivable audience other than that of his peers and no overt relevance to the major problems of our time. The most effective and successful disciplines are those which combine both pure and applied interests in the same body of scholars. The continuing exchange between pure and applied provides, not only a sense of relevance and purpose, but in the long run a strategy for the discipline as a whole.

Obviously there are no easy answers to questions about the functions of universities and learned societies, no simple programmatic solutions to the problem of the

appropriate institutional framework for education, research and service. But clearly learned societies have
both opportunities and responsibilities to relieve some of
the burdens thrust upon universities. As societies rather
than complex institutions, they have less inertia, fewer
vested interests and no formal public responsibilities.
They may have a special mission at a stage in history
when our most valuable resource is knowledge and our
most difficult problem relates to its use.

John Voss
Executive Officer
American Academy of Arts
and Sciences

CONTENTS

INTRODUCTION
ACADEMIES AND ACADEMIA

IN THE EARLY summer of 1969 a small group of men and women, all concerned in one way or another with institutions of higher education and with other learned societies, met for three pleasant days beside an Adirondack lake and talked about recent troubles in American universities, about what those troubles portended for the future, and generally about learned societies in an age of confrontation. This little book grew out of those talks. Its constituent essays pretend to no comprehensive statistical support. No ingenious electronic device fed its pages with mystic computations. Our book purports only to give the thoughts suggested to some intelligent

xxiii

people in a few rare hours of leisure, by talking about matters which greatly concern them. This sort of reflective interchange is not frequent, which is perhaps the best justification for giving it permanent form.

To the American Council of Learned Societies and the American Academy of Arts and Sciences go the thanks of contributors and editors for making these talks possible. To Syracuse University they are indebted for the use of its Sagamore Lake outpost, where during a few June days the only confrontations facing visitors were the timid advances of eleven mendicant deer.

I The Idea of an Academy and the Causes of Confrontation

American colleges, academies, universities, and such associations of learned men as the Modern Language Association, are the institutions discussed in these essays. A few sentences, putting in perspective these several varieties of academic establishments, are probably useful. Our colleges originated one supposes as purely teaching establishments; witness, in the seventeenth century Harvard and William and Mary. Eighteenth-century "academies" such as the American Philosophical Society and the American Academy of Arts and Sciences were organizations of thoughtful men, most of them not "academics" in the modern sense. These Fellows were at once intellectuals and busy men of affairs—John Adams, Benjamin Franklin and the like. They organized

xxiv

such societies to exchange, by writing and by speech, news of scientific discoveries, of ingenuous speculations about society, of philosophy in its original meaning.

Universities in America grew up after 1865, though several institutions bore that name much earlier. A university in our usage of the term combines the function of the teaching college and that of the academy, both functions intensified by phenomenal technological advance. The colleges of 1650-1850, which taught a few young men a rather simple and uniform system of mathematical, classical, and philosophical lore, evolved after 1865 into much larger institutions which, to be sure, undertook to teach, to those who sought them, the early established curricula, but which in addition undertook to teach a bewildering array of occupational arts—medicine, law, engineering, agriculture, dozens of others. Related to these latter, underlying them and dependent on them, grew up "pure" as distinguished from "applied" scientific learning. The meaning of the adjective "pure" is difficult to perceive. The term occurs more frequently governing scientific "research" than the teaching of science. Here some scanning of the term "research" is necessary. It is a process in, say, literature quite different from that in physics or astronomy. Perhaps, however, a trait common to all research is its primary purpose of discovery, assembly, or rearrangement of facts or ideas, rather than the transmission to students of facts or ideas already available. The American university undertook teaching and research together.

As it developed, the university assumed many of the

functions of a classic "academy." It assembled a company of scholars who exchanged ideas in writing or in print, as the fellows of the academies did in their days of origin. The university scholars met at lunch, and in the laboratory and the seminar, in a sort of continuous academy meeting. Some few of these scholars engaged in research at the expense of some teaching; a very few even carried on research to the point that they did no instructing. Some institutions grew up having no function other than that of research, part of them governmental, others industrial, a few like the Brookings Institution neither the one nor the other.

After 1865 along with the rise of universities in America there grew up a number of associations each devoted to some specific field of learning, drawing most of its membership from university and college faculties. Such were the American Historical Association (1884), the Modern Language Association (1883), the American Philological Association (1869). By 1910 there were approximately 35 such organizations. They grew up contemporaneously with the growth of American universities, which stimulated their origin. These learned societies served two separate purposes. They fostered substantive learning and publications in their several journals or in hard-cover volumes or both. They held annual gatherings at which their members, coming from many colleges and universities, presented and discussed papers on topics of their research, thus serving the principal functions of eighteenth-century academies. In addition they came to perform occupational service functions for their members, notably providing means for young scholars available for academic employment to meet department chairmen at colleges and universities which needed teachers.

More recently such learned societies have assembled themselves in federations, loosely organized according to related subject matter. The American Council of Learned Societies, one such federation, accepts member organizations generally associated with "the humanities," insofar as that amorphous term identifies any field of human concern. Scientists, biological and others, have affiliated their component societies with the American Academy of Sciences. These agglomerate societies support publications and sponsor discussions on subjects common to their component members. In that respect they approach even closer to the functions of the earlier Academies.

In the post-World War II period, American higher education began to expand, and its growth continues at a dizzying rate of acceleration, especially in public institutions. State universities multiplied their facilities, state colleges became universities, many private institutions were incorporated into state systems, and a national movement saw the creation of hundreds of two-year community colleges. The students came, with every variety of anticipation and aspiration, including millions from families for whom college education had been an impossible dream. The Federal Government encouraged attendance when it began support to military veterans and programs of student loans, educational opportunity grants, work-study payments, and a massive array of graduate fellowships. By the fall of 1968 the total enrollment of degree-credit students was 6.98 million; by curious coincidence, the U.S. Census Bureau Current Population Survey of March, 1968, estimated that of the total population twenty-five years or older, 6.98 million had completed four years of college.

In the later 1960s, for reasons not altogether clear, a curious malaise swept through many students in many universities in many parts of the world. Students organized protests, made "demands," seized and held university buildings to curricular ransom, and accused university authorities of grievous shortcomings. In the United States much of the discontent focused on the war in Vietnam, and on the universities' supposed cooperation in its conduct by training reserve military officers, and by fostering scientific research on materials and devices useful in that war. Sometimes protest extended to a university's corporate failure to denounce the war or to refuse cooperation with military conscription. And war was not the only American grievance. Some protest was directed against growth of urban universities which, the protestors thought, inevitably displaced poor folk who had lived where the universities built new hospitals or laboratories. In some instances black students, and some white as well, protested against the universities' failure to provide "relevant" programs of "black studies," taught by blacks whom blacks selected.

These purported grievances were not, one feels, the fundamental causes of disaffection; the true causes probably lay much deeper. The bright promise of the eighteenth century, offering democratic felicity to all mankind if only man would strike off the chains in which tyranny held him—that promise fell in default when man struck off the chains, emancipated the general will, and found himself still subject to the tyranny of the majority which he found as unsatisfactory as whatever system had preceded. In America successive generations were told in election after election that they were governed by rascals whom, so aspiring politicians urged, the new voters should turn out by installing rulers of the opposition party. When the overthrow came, it brought less than alabaster cities; human tears continued. Politics was oversold.

The same oversell went on in education. Under elms and in front of June ivy, graduating class after graduating class heard eminent men tell the rising generation, generation after generation, that its elders had failed, that the only hope of a decent world lay with the young men and women there assembled in academic costume. Sooner or later some of them were bound to believe this, particularly because this combined denunciation and promise was partly true. Clearly the old do give way; the young do succeed them; and university graduates do, by and large, determine national policy. The result has not been utopia.

On June 12, 1969, a candidate for a degree in law delivered one of the historic Harvard Commencement Parts, on the theme that "confrontation" by contemporary college and university students resulted from their taking their professors seriously. Campus revolts, he seemed to tell his hearers, resulted from doctrines which educators expounded but to which they only half-subscribed, while their young disciples believed and hoped. With due allowance for a certain oversimplification, the young man still expressed a view which had some rational cogency. Civilization is indeed in a sorry state; and little comfort comes from a reminder that this state of affairs has always obtained. The brute fact confronts our habit of boastful optimism. "We Americans can do anything on which we set our minds and hearts," we like to tell ourselves. We have poverty programs; vast plans for universal education; model-cities plans. But poverty persists; education falters; cities are hardly models. Our military efforts in southeast Asia have not brought peace and justice there. We hoped for great things from the United Nations; but most of our hopes are disappointed, and a well-intending ambassador we send finds difficulty in making good-will visits to South American nations. Civilization is not an unqualified success and we can scarcely fault idealistic young students for recognizing this. They are, however, hardly justified in harming their colleges and universities because civilization is unsatisfactory. They will not improve our academic institutions if they make them organs of political pressure rather than societies for scholarly endeavor. But dissatisfaction is real, and not alone among the young. Its consequences for scholarly institutions well deserved our conversations at Sagamore Lake.

Arthur Sutherland

CIVILITY AND CIVILIZATION

Arthur E. Sutherland

ONE WHO UNDERTAKES to discuss the role of a learned society in a time of confrontation at once finds himself plagued by the elusive meaning of words. A time of "confrontation?"

As the term appears in any discussion of today's universities where the phenomenon has lately been most abundant, it seems to mean the posture of a group of people, mostly undergraduates, who feel aggrieved, who are emotionally moved by a sense that what they want is right, and that by an ineluctible logic of opposites whoever withholds concurrence is therefore wrong. Confrontation, in current usage, assumes that the process of reason has somehow ceased to function. Those who might normally be expected to mend their erring ways on the showing made by their young admonishers but who stubbornly do not, are at best stupidly backward or worse are consciously corrupt. Reason, having failed to persuade to rectitude or to dissuade from wrong those in power, failed even to rouse inert bystanders to join the movement; forcible action must replace mere dialogue or the better cause will lie in the dust.

This intellectual posture of confrontation, I hasten to suggest, is not confined to any historical era, doctrine, social class or institution. In 1782 Lord North sent a note to George III concerning the position of the Opposition in the Commons. The King sent back North's letter endorsed

I have no wish but the prosperity of my dominions; therefore must look upon all who would not heartily assist me as bad men, as well as ungrateful subjects.

Thackeray in *The Four Georges* paraphrased this, "I wish nothing but good, therefore every man who does not agree with me is a traitor and a scoundrel."

"Confrontation" today has become a word of art. Cardinal to it is this complete, unshakable conviction of rightness on the part of the activists, deep belief in the necessity of action now if wrong is not to triumph. Similarly inherent is the exasperated loss of faith in rational persuasion. "Come now, and let us reason together" has become mere vanity and vexation of spirit, for in the faculty and administration there is no vision and the students perish. The language of the Old Testament prophets at once comes to mind, for in those who confront burns much of the prophet's messianic flame. Recession from righteous demands is for them inconceivable; some causes are not negotiable; some compromises of principle, they tell us, no decent man will ask or give.

Indeed some human aspirations are not tradable. Some principles are so sacred that patriots or martyrs will refuse to compromise with conscience. We have made national heroes of men who turned to violence as the only remaining way. Every American schoolboy knows, or at any rate used to know, that the Bostonians who threw British tea in the harbor were right, that they acted in a noble cause. To the abolitionists of the 1850s antislavery was a righteous crusade justifying violent resistance against wicked laws. In 1861 thousands of young men marched away to a war against brethren, singing "John Brown's Body" to strengthen their hearts. They sang to canonize a fiercely righteous man who for a cause he had embraced killed other men in Bleeding Kansas and who, seizing a federal arsenal as the only way to strike an effective blow against slavery, led his own sons to death at Harper's Ferry and was himself hanged there. Amid much shocked outcry against Brown's insurrection, Ralph Waldo Emerson's voice rang out, "That new saint . . . will make the gallows glorious like the cross." Three years later Julia Ward Howe welcomed the tune of "John Brown's Body" for her "Battle Hymn of the Republic."

For many generations at Harvard, students have shared in the commencement ritual by presenting Commencement Parts, short speeches, one in Latin, two in English, written by those who successfully compete for the privilege. In June 1969, a young man gave such an address concerning the commitments to liberal causes to which he and his classmates had been converted during their college years, and their expectations after student days. His words were eloquent, and I was much moved. I venture to quote part.

In short, we will have to face our consciences. Many of us will discover conflicts between our desire for personal success and the values we have espoused as students. It will not be enough merely to vocalize our values. To do so is to be guilty of the same kind of hypocrisy which we have denounced in others. Belief without action accomplished nothing. We must act. The responsibility for change is fast becoming our burden.

It can be said of this class that we protested against injustice and discrimination, and we were right.

We demanded an end to poverty, and we were right.

We refused to accept an unjust war, and we were right.

We sought changes in an academic system which was losing touch with the times, and we were right.

Let us hope that in the future it can be said of us that we refused to accept our society as it was, and instead, worked to make it closer to what it can be, because that too will be right.

The young orator spoke earnestly. At each "We were right," he raised his voice in a defiantly hortatory cry. After his climax of continued rightness, amid well-deserved applause from the thousands in his audience, he gravely bowed to the President, and walked down the steps, off into what I knew would be a future of much valiant effort, and of many lessons still to learn. For I was sure that no one in his audience favored any of the wrongs he so rightly condemned—discrimination, poverty, unjust warfare, or an academic system out of touch with the times. But as there is little self-stimulus in a defiant statement of what everybody in hearing already favors, I felt that the boy was romantically picturing himself as one who throws down the gage before a strong enemy, as young David with only a sling and smooth stones from the brook, confronting Goliath of Gath, as one of the seven against great Thebes. All the frustrating problems of means, adjustment, compromise, delay which go with any reform achieved by democratic procedure in which there are selfish or short-sighted men still entitled to votes, and men of good will who advocate different remedies, all these he overlooked; and for sympathetic understanding of others, he substituted a sort of *"j'accuse,"* a denigration of verbal persuasion and in its place a call to some unspecified action. In justice to our student orator I point out that he was not a participant in the forcible seizure of Harvard's University Hall. I quote him because his statement so well expresses the spirit of the time, the political theory of confrontation.

Another young man, though denied his degree because of his active involvement, still at his classmates' request was allowed to address the Commencement audience. He sounded quite a different note.

> . . . In fact, Harvard is run by the men who profit from the things we oppose—the Vietnam war, racism, slums, the lies people are taught. In plain English, Harvard is used by the very rich to screw the very poor. When we fight Harvard, we are not "raising issues" or making moral protests—rather, we are fighting to STOP the very real and ferocious attacks Harvard, in the service to the men who run it, makes on the people of the world every day. . . .
>
> . . . We will not retreat into diversionary reasoning with these men who need to defeat all movements against their interests. We will not be

intimidated by the small dose of repression we've been handed. We will not be discouraged by the press' distortions of our movement. Our seizure of University Hall has been punished! The punishment palls beside the punishments workers especially Blacks receive all the time—e.g. the Panthers in New Haven who have been framed for ritual murder. But that seizure is also mild compared to what the people are going to do to the rulers!

Perhaps we might well remind ourselves that American learned societies have lived through a long train of confrontations. The American Philosophical Society, born at Philadelphia in 1743, saw the development of our quarrels with Britain, heard the debates over independence, felt the long agony of revolutionary war. In 1780, the year when the American cause reached its nadir, John Adams and a group of his Boston friends organized the American Academy of Arts and Sciences. Both societies must have shared the pain of the country's division between patriots and loyalists. A large number of our fellow Americans joined loyalist regiments and fought against the revolutionary forces; some civilian loyalists left their homes and took refuge in New York or other British-held parts of the thirteen colonies, or went to Canada. The bitterness of that confrontation, now found only in history books, was tragic at the time. The Treaty of 1783 gave loyalists a right to reclaim their confiscated American lands, and when in 1793 the

Supreme Court took jurisdiction of such a suit, the *Massachusetts Mercury* fulminated against the plaintiff, ". . . If he should obtain what he has sued for, what a wide extended door will it open for every dirty Tory traitor to his country's liberties to enter." The hostile alignment over the Alien and Sedition Acts; New England's antagonism against the War of 1812; the controversies over the Fugitive Slave Law, which once caused the Harvard Corporation to veto a professor's appointment; the Copperhead movement in the northern states between 1861 and 1865; all have the characteristics of confrontation; abandonment of persuasion, marshalling of irreconcible groups ready to take violent measures each against the other. The bitter labor controversies which marred the last two decades of the nineteenth century; the anti-Germanism of 1917 which at Harvard brought a painful social ostracism on Professor Hugo Munsterberg; the Espionage Act prosecutions of 1918, which could generate threats among Harvard's Overseers against the tenure of a professor who criticized the convictions; all these were "confrontations" in their antithetical alignments according to emotional, hardened commitments transcending reasoned debate. So were the race riots of 1919. So were some of the political and social controversies over the New Deal; so was the McCarthy anticommunist deployment of the 1940s and 1950s.

But one wonders how far Berkeley, Columbia, Harvard, Cornell, and the others in 1969 really resemble the

Britain of George III and of General Gates; the slave owners enforcing the Fugitive Slave Act; Pinkerton strike breakers of three generations ago; McCarthy's anticommunist allies. Will future historians find that today's fierce young men with their grievances against their several seminaries of learning were justified in violence because their demands were not granted? Are colleges and universities academically or morally barred from using the public force to resist forcible distraint of their premises or of their officers? Unfortunately, no rule of thumb, no book of reference can now answer these questions to the satisfaction of everybody. Ultimately, we face here, as elsewhere, the baffling choice between right and wrong; and in some cases only time delivers judgment, as it has in favor of the loyalists of the 1780s and the fugitive slaves of the 1850s. Will the college captors someday be justified as we now justify the Bostonians who poured out the British tea chests, or John Brown who under fire of the Marines briefly held the engine house at Harper's Ferry?

All of today's learned societies have lived through some confrontations, and some of the societies have lived through all I have mentioned. A study of the reaction of those societies to those divisions of opinion and emotion would perhaps be enlightening, perhaps yield nothing. At any rate, it is beyond the bounds of time and strength available for this essay. But obviously the present discontents are unprecedented in some respects. The world has never seen so great a proportion of a

11

large nation's young men and women spending their years of early maturity in seminaries of learning. The recent widespread campus unhappiness and disorders evidence a new dissatisfaction felt by a large number of students with their teachers and with the general conduct of their centers of learning, a sense that seminaries of learning are neglecting their duty to improve the sad state of human society. I hasten to say that the power of colleges and universities to right the world's wrongs is much less than some of my young friends think; that neglect of these wrongs on our campuses is by no means as great as they estimate; that discontent with the state of higher learning is not as pervasive among students as its most vocal exponents tell us. Hyperbole is an American folkway not limited to the political and advertising arts. But existence of widespread and sometimes violent discontent is a brute fact, regardless of its justification. A certain number (or better, an uncertain number) of our young people persuade themselves that they could manage matters better, and anyhow the customer is always right and ought to control fashions in what he studies as he does in the clothes he buys.

The wisdom of applying this merchandising maxim to higher education is at least questionable. Pressed with sufficient vigor, it could turn our universities into political societies, giant caucuses, disorderly guilds, asserting unconvincingly that their majoritarian syndics are single-hearted in search for truth. Examples have existed in

European universities of past ages; they exist today in some countries. Their advertising value is low.

What should, or can, American learned societies do in the face of this horrid prospect? Nowhere else in the world are there so many societies of learned men united by their common interests in various fields of intellectual endeavor, but without bodies of young students to take the field against their elders. Surely, one might feel, here must be a great militia for a parlous time. On the day of Armageddon shall we tarry by the stuff? Shall we be sluggards, dreaming in our closets while others fight on this Saint Crispin's Day?

Well, yes. On the whole I suggest that as societies we stay a little removed from this one. There is little good we are equipped to accomplish by contentious involvement and much harm that may come of the attempt. Surely we would make a futile display if we adopted corporate resolutions admonishing one side or the other in the campus wars, or both sides, to abandon the barricades and return to the trivial round, the common task. I suppose few men ever think nowadays of the Ford Peace Ship of 1914 and its company of well-meaning but somewhat impractical folk who embarked for newly embattled Europe inspired by their slogan, "Out of the trenches by Christmas!" and by the belief that if only the combatant governments heard their reasoned arguments for peace they would all lay down their arms. People who are nerved to battle do not listen to reason.

The trouble with confrontation is precisely its psychological likeness to angry and self-righteous warfare, while the mode of the scholarly society, one hopes, is receptivity to ideas in a spirit of gracious civility. But the scholar's inconclusive balance between two doubts is uncomfortable in a nation suffused with confident zeal, tending to certainty that it knows what is right and can bring it about, just as it bridged the rivers, tamed the wilderness, and set brave men on the moon who brought back pieces of it. The open mind suggests that quite possibly there is much to be said for the other fellow; but full, unquestioning, single-minded commitment to one's own righteous cause is zealous, heady, rousing, inspiriting. We Americans dislike debatable issues; they bewilder us. Kipling in 1894 wrote of this trait in "An American"—

> . . . dazed by many doubts he wakes
> The drumming guns that—have no doubts.

We wake drumming guns on many a metaphorical front. We make "war on crime" which saves us from unwelcome and embarrassing questions as to what "crime" is. We wage "war on drugs," "war on cancer," "war on pollution," "war on poverty,"—all "campaigns" that can tolerate no qualms. No one, surely, has pity for cancer or pollution or poverty. *Écrasez l'infâme!* Fund-raisers, over the top!

For many centuries Christian men have sung battle

hymns to hearten them in their warfare against evil, hymns like

> Christian up and smith them
> Counting gain but loss. . . .

or

> Onward Christian soldiers
> Marching as to war . . .
> Forward into battle
> See, his banners go.

I sing these old rousing songs with more satisfaction than I intone some of the more sophisticated and less martial ones. Legions of men share this musical evocation of adrenaline. Was it not the young Roman officer in *Androcles and the Lion* who, marching a band of Christians off to the place of execution, rebuked their leader for the seditious sentiments of "Onward Christian Soldiers?" He observed, however, that the prisoners seemed to march the better for the song, and suggested that they sing less obnoxious words to the same tune. As an example he sang, 'Throw them to the li–ons.'

Even the dictionary definition of confrontation has an etymology rooted in warfare. "Confront. To face, esp. hostilely." To face as an enemy, that is. One must confront social and governmental evils, prepared to smite them hip and thigh, not to discuss their possible justification. A student friend of mine once told me that we professors sometimes made classrooms intolerable by our "on the one hand, but then again on the other" manner of discussing what the student found crying wrongs; sometimes, he said he had to leave the lecture hall from sheer frustration. There was much to be said for this young man; why be tolerant of the devil when you are sure of his identity? There are, of course, collateral consequences of this. Let us suppose, for example, that I am a student who deeply opposes the real-estate policies of my University; it is, I am convinced, brutally taking the dwellings of the poor in order to build laboratories and the like. Some professor or administrator contends that the land is better used for needed health services. The wretched fellow is siding with the enemy! I must extend my hate to him and his laboratory, for he has made himself an accomplice of evil, he is a deserter in the war against poverty.

Some professions are inconsistent with self-questioning. Their votaries can enjoy the luxury of certitude. Successful evangelists do not gain converts by preaching of their own doctrinal waverings. Fund-raisers must not express doubts of the merits of the charities for which they bespeak largesse. If copywriters for advertising agencies are ever beset by doubts as to the merits of their merchandise these qualms do not emerge in their prose. I have rarely, if ever, heard a political orator weigh the demerits of his own candidate against his virtues and conclude that on the whole he was probably a better man than his adversary. Indeed one of the most successful stump-speakers this country has ever known used so to delight his adherents by talented and unmixed denunciation of adversaries that when he paused for breath the eager crowd would shout "Pour it on Harry!"

But the thinker functions best, we like to tell ourselves, when he is continually reexamining his premises. Justice Holmes in 1897, when he had been fourteen years on the Massachusetts Supreme Judicial Court, spoke of fundamental questions which "still await a better answer than that we do as our fathers have done," and asked "What have we better than a blind guess to show that the criminal law in its present form does more good than harm?" In 1915 he wrote "To have doubted one's own first principles is the mark of a civilized man." And in companies of scholars this weighing of doubt flourishes best when the concourse is graced by civility, when the other man's expressions are heard with kindness, when doubt is not an insult.

This sort of gracious talk is quite unrelated to majoritarianism of opinion. Common-room conversation would not be improved if when Jones ventured an opinion on something, Smith called for a vote of those present to determine the correctness of Jones' view. And for similar reasons I am reluctant to see my own Society take a majority vote on a debated question of public moment. If opinion is divided, the minority is uneasily quieted, and if the papers hear of the result, a misleading appearance emerges that there is an official view.

"But," I can hear some one say, "in the learned

societies are large assemblies of intelligent men and women, and in the campus confrontations appears a movement which might by transforming our universities, deeply affect the intellectual life of the United States. That these societies should ignore them is ridiculous." With this I quite agree. My own Academy through its various committees is continually examining public questions, discussing them in papers or orally or both, and often printing the papers in its Quarterly, *Daedelus*, or in other publications. I draw a clear distinction between the expressed thought of an individual and anything approaching a corporate statement of a society, determined by majority vote leaving the dissenters somewhat abashed. I should welcome, in my own Society, a study, by committee, of the general question of student participation in the government of universities, the history of such participation in the past, its observed performance in the present where it occurs, and a prediction of its future. But when these papers are printed I would be sorry to see a vote of the Fellows to determine the orthodox view. The vote would not fix truth.

Universities and colleges are fragile creations. The best in them is a kindliness of coexistence, a noncontentious tolerance, civility; and this, the essential ingredient of civilization, immediately disappears in a state of war. The fearsome passage of Hobbes put it three centuries and more ago:

Whatsoever therefore is consequent to a time of

Warre, where every man is Enemy to every man; the same is consequent to the time, wherein men live without other security, that what their own strength, and their own invention shall furnish them withall. In such condition, there is no place for Industry; because the fruit thereof is uncertain: and consequently no Culture of the Earth; no Navigation, nor use of the commodities that may be imported by Sea; no commodious Building; no Instruments of moving, and removing such things as require much force; no Knowledge of the face of the Earth; no account of Time; no Arts; no Letters; no Society; and which is worst of all, continuall fears, and danger of violent death; And the life of man, solitary, poore, nasty, brutish, and short.

If by confrontation some group in a university insists on intestine war to gain its objectives, the university will lose its civility, its essential nature, and its best capability to advance civilization. The inevitable incursion of counterforce, of police, can not restore lost civility any more than a court decree can restore a marriage. In the face of confrontation the university is damned if it does and damned if it does not. Its essence is consensual, like all the best relations in man's existence. Confrontation has put it in peril of its life.

The role of learned societies in time of confrontation, then, might be rephrased as the role of learned societies if the civility of the university, as we have known it, should disappear. There might still be lectures, examinations, some learning, degrees. But the easiness, the sense of common purpose, unselfishness that so far as I know has existed in the same degree in no other institutions of our time, most of these would go. The intellectual fertility deriving from these would go from our universities. Possibly much could still survive in learned societies. All Souls College has long existed without students. We might spend more time in our societies as faculty club tables and the common rooms become less comfortable. Learned societies cannot stop disaster in our colleges if students insist on confrontation. If that disaster continues, Societies may be new custodians of civility and civilization.

UNIVERSITY REFORM AND
THE PROBLEM OF
"RELEVANT" SCHOLARSHIP *

Michael R. Winston

* I wish to acknowledge the helpful criticisms of this essay
by Dr. John Voss, American Academy of Arts and Sciences, and
Dr. Conrad K. Harper, Legal Defense and Educational Fund, Inc.

THE ASSAULT ON universities by disaffected students and reactionary politicians has been one of the most tragic and ugly features of the current social and political crisis gripping the United States. The spectacle of university campuses which have symbolized the civilizing values of higher learning, overwhelmed by violent clashes between demonstrating students and helmeted police became a major part of the image of higher education in the late 1960s. Public confidence in universities was eroded, and the various constituencies within them, especially stu-

23

dents and faculty, faced each other in an atmosphere of deepening distrust. Proliferating suspicions were not directed merely at the motives of particular students, faculty or administrators, but also at the enterprise of higher education itself, its institutional structure, fundamental purposes, and, more broadly, its social and cultural consequences. Conventional campus punditry generally maintains that this state of affairs flows principally from the unhappy juxtaposition of fundamentally incompatible, sclerotic social institutions and the heightened moral sensibilities of the young. It is usually argued that angry students alienated by the moral defects of a technocratic, repressive society, have collided with faculty and administrators representing the established order, who allege interest in the preservation of traditional values and the integrity of the university as a center for free inquiry and intellectual exchange.

For all of its obvious oversimplification, this conflict model of American campuses does serve a useful function by bringing into sharp relief the basic polarities of the situation. A new generation of college students, spurred by the example of the civil rights movement and horrified by the war in Vietnam, has rejected a society which can harbor squalor in the shadows of its affluence, can nurture racism while trumpeting its democratic ideals, and expend billions on armaments and war in the name of world peace. For a variety of reasons, universities have become a social battleground, incarnating for many students the corruption of reason, its

24

lofty ideals merely a hypocritical mask for sinister, even inhuman research enterprises on behalf of the military and giant corporations. In contrast, some within the university could legitimately view the chronic manifestations of student unrest, particularly the sometimes violent disruption of teaching, as the greatest single threat to the future of the university. It is this collision, between morally outraged students and professors genuinely concerned with the future of unfettered intellectual inquiry, which is most complex and painful.

The irony of this situation is that the present crisis is as much a result of the virtues of the American university as of its defects. In the United States there developed over a period of years a conception of the character and function of universities quite different from British or continental European models, despite sporadic efforts in the nineteenth century to import, especially from Germany, particular patterns of graduate training and research. What may loosely be called the "American conception" of the university grew quite naturally out of American conditions, notably the circumstance of being a "developing nation" a century ago, and America's profession of democratic ideals. This view, at once liberal and pragmatic, held that the university must be both a center of scholarly inquiry and a community "service" institution, as well as opening its doors to a far higher percentage of the young than European universities. State universities are probably the most complete expression of this idea, where the prac-

25

tical needs of agriculture and industry have been usually regarded as having the same quality of legitimacy in the institution as the more traditional functions of teaching and scholarship. With the passage of time, a broad spectrum of activities was incorporated within an expanding circle of institutional concerns, ranging from efforts to automate crop harvesting to the development of new weapons for the military. A bewildering thicket of "programs," community service projects, institutes for applied research, and training workshops, became a part of what was to be denominated the "multiversity." It is not at all surprising that an institution so vaguely defined, and comprehending so many activities as the contemporary American university should find itself vulnerable and misunderstood. It is also undoubtedly true that the peculiar American variant of the Western university has been spectacularly successful in serving an extraordinary range of economic, social, and cultural needs; but this success has in turn generated expectations, often contradictory, which cannot be met by any single social institution.

In response to the disastrous spasms of student disruption and faculty reaction of recent years, much energy is being expended on projecting the future of universities, teaching, and research. From much of the current discussion about these matters there is emerging one thought in particular which has failed to stimulate the kind of scrutiny it deserves. This is the notion, by now a commonplace in some institutions, that the solution to our present dilemma on the campuses, resides in making universities, in all important respects, "relevant" to the needs of society. Since many within and without the university view the present crisis as deriving from a *lack* of university response to social problems, there is a seductive simplicity to the proposition that universities become directly engaged in their solution. In accord with this general assumption, there has been a remarkable increase in university-related enterprises directed at specific social problems as conceived by government bureaucrats, foundation executives, trustees, and professors. Examples readily come to mind: university centers for urban research and planning, institutes for environmental studies, or more conventionally, training programs sponsored by government social welfare agencies. The tacit assumption underlying this trend is that university research in such matters is "neutral." But it is increasingly evident that mission-oriented social research and policy studies are indeed shrouded by a host of issues involving not only questions of value, but also of political power. Solutions to problems of environmental pollution, housing development, or traffic control, for example, all involve questions of costs and benefits to particular social groups, defying all attempts, no matter how sincere, to be "neutral." Thus, socially "relevant" research enterprises in universities are no more likely to avoid the fundamental problem involved in military research, erosion of the university's position as a nonpartisan center for inquiry. It should be under-

27

stood that I am not arguing for an avoidance of investigation into controversial questions, for that would entail a betrayal of the commitment to critical thought. The point is more restricted. It is that universities should not confuse inquiry with research enterprises which entail advocacy of particular solutions to social problems because this stimulates a political process destructive of the most precious asset of the university, its *authority*. "Irrelevance" or "relevance" seem to be very clumsy, inadequate terms in any discussion of matters as complex as the proper degree to which universities should involve themselves in the needs of societies which support them.

It is demonstrably clear that universities have in many instances suffered precisely because of their "relevance." To some, classified research in universities is unpalatable; but military research is, after all, "relevant." Within faculty ranks, the matter very often degenerates to the level of "my relevant project is better than yours." For some political conservatives in the university, "relevant" military research is acceptable because it is useful for the defense and security of the nation, while "relevant" social action research is not. The demands for relevance derive directly from the misunderstanding of the "natural limits" of an institution like a university. As I indicated earlier, the peculiar American variant of the university was particularly vulnerable to overextension and confusion because of the lack of specificity in its conception of itself. Any attempt to unscramble the now almost hopelessly tangled, and often contradictory,

28

functions of American universities must, however, take into account the vastly changed role of knowledge and large-scale organization in a "postindustrial" technocratic state.

The new importance of knowledge to economic and political systems has consequences which, although profound, have been for the most part ignored by the academic community. In the last thirty years certain branches of knowledge have become crucial to the success of business corporations, military enterprises, economic and social planning, and the operation of government. Universities assumed a new kind of importance and influence largely unrelated to their conventional educative functions. The change in the level of financial support for basic and applied research is just one small indication of the new position of American universities as strategic centers for generating useful new knowledge. In 1940, for example, American colleges and universities were spending 50 million dollars on research; virtually all of it was basic research funded by the institutions themselves. By 1960, the research bill at American universities had risen to 1.2 billion dollars; half of this was in the field of applied research, and the Federal Government was supplying 75 percent of all research funds. This startling change, both in the volume and scope of university research, also modified important relationships, principally between universities and government, and between increasingly differentiated constituencies within universities. Within a short span of time, the substance

29

of universities' independence was substantially eroded by a growing financial dependence on the Federal Government. Many of the nation's most prestigious universities were involved, some more deeply than others, in classified research on weapons systems, chemical and biological warfare, counterinsurgency techniques, and a host of other projects scarcely conceivable twenty-five years ago. Generally, it was not until an articulate minority of concerned students began to protest that these research enterprises had no place in a university, that most universities began to review seriously their propriety in a community of scholars. This fact alone is indicative of a major part of the problem. Universities had so broadened their activities that the old corporate ideal of a "community of scholars" had been sacrificed, no doubt inadvertently, and only a small minority within the university could agree on criteria for a judgment of what activities were "legitimate" in a company of scholars. It is of course true, as some university apologists for military research have argued, that classified research, even when concentrated in large laboratories associated with universities (for example, the Lincoln Laboratory at M.I.T. or the Lawrence Radiation Laboratory at Berkeley), is a very small part of the total research effort at American universities. In almost all cases, the argument goes, defense-related research has had virtually no effect on other research areas, undergraduate curricula, or the academic freedom of faculty and students. All of this may be true, but it misses the

30

crucial point, which is essentially moral, involving the largely ignored issue of the ethical boundaries of applied research. This issue cannot be responded to in terms of quantities; the whole university enterprise is compromised by that small part devoted to partisan purposes.

Because of the pivotal role of knowledge in advanced societies, there have developed new pressures for its social control, organization, and utilization, so that specific goals may be achieved. This has had the effect of generating a process which may loosely be called the "politicization" of knowledge. This process threatens to destroy utterly the integrity of the academic world. Scholars and universities are in crisis not so much for ignoring social pressures that their work be "relevant," but because they have chosen to serve causes that have lost the support of a substantial minority in society, particularly the young. Thus, association with the Institute for Defense Analyses, Project Camelot, the Department of Defense, and sundry other "relevant" organizations has compromised the university's (and by extension the scholar's) claim to engage in the disinterested pursuit of truth. If scholarship is to preserve its authority, it must dissociate itself from power. It is ironic that so many in the academic world have seen dissident students as a greater threat to scholarship than the incursions of politicized research. Scholars have themselves to blame largely for the disarray of academe. The responsibility for preserving the integrity of scholarship rests with scholars, despite the fact that university administrators

ordinarily have the statutory power to undertake contracts and associations in the name of the university. A
reordering of priorities is necessary in universities, as
well as a careful examination of the relationships between
teaching, scholarship, applied research, and community
service. Unfortunately, much of the discussion to date
has been dominated by cant like the "generation gap,"
"multiversity versus university," and "publish or perish,"
which obscures rather than clarifies fundamental
problems.

My own experience of campus turbulence, although
confined to a relatively short period of time, has been
intensified and yet broadened by the circumstance of my
changing roles—student, faculty member, and academic
administrator—during one of the academic world's most
turbulent periods. The modest proposals that follow are
frankly the product of this experience, and probably
reflect the dismay anyone feels who has witnessed at
close range the torment of campuses reduced to one of
the major battlegrounds of our society. First, I think it
is imperative that universities divest themselves of all
classified research projects. In addition, all those applied
research projects and institutes (on highways, alcoholism,
or interior decorating) which do not contribute directly
to the academic purposes of the university should be
abandoned. Military research must be eliminated, not
because it is unimportant or that it is unpopular with
dissident students and faculty, but because it has nothing to do with free inquiry and truth. It compromises

universities politically, inevitably creates an atmosphere destructive to open investigation and destroys one of the foundations of academic life—a sense of mutual trust between members of the academic community. This type of research can be carried on in government laboratories and institutes especially designed for this purpose, like the Rocky Mountain Center for CBW research; there is no justification for universities to assume these burdens. Applied, nonmilitary research in universities is a more complicated problem. Some of this work is closely related to some major problems of importance to scholars, such as the many institutes devoted to "area studies," which are of interest to historians, geographers, linguists, economists, and others. They are, among other things, useful organizational devices for breaking down the numerous artificial barriers between scholarly disciplines. Thus they are valuable to inquiry, and facilitate the work of scholars. Their exploitation by government agencies, however, should be stopped because "policy studies" compromise the academic world's integrity, although in an admittedly more subtle manner than military research. Technical institutes, engineering projects, and community service programs present equally thorny questions. Most engineering schools and technical institutes in the United States are part of universities. The very nature of the fields concerned requires involvement of the institution in a very broad spectrum of activities. Given the growing size of these enterprises, however, it is probable that they should

33

become fully independent organizations, especially if the majority of the work conducted is not related to instruction. Community service programs similarly ought to be conducted independently when their activity is remote from teaching or basic research, even though these programs are consistent with the service dimension of the "American university idea." It is not at all clear that universities are the best vehicles for social programs, despite the obvious fact that much of the "expertise" required for their success is presently concentrated in universities.

Two major shifts in the organization and structure of centers for knowledge are implicit in the proposal for universities to divest themselves of all organized research enterprises not directly related to their *academic* purposes. One change would be a radical redefinition of the university's role in American society. It would entail a narrowing of the range of university activities, mainly by eliminating the ties to agriculture, industry, and government. By dropping their role as "knowledge conglomerates" universities will be better able to serve the highest needs of a free society, genuine freedom of intellectual inquiry, and institutions which sustain and protect criticism and creativity. Such freedom has costs, principally a loss of funds for large-scale research projects, and a resulting decline in the "prestige" deriving from association with power. Our rhetoric of "community service" has been both too vague and lacking in vision, resulting in the wild assortment of projects which reduce the university to society's intellectual handyman, an all purpose fix-it shop. While society undoubtedly needs such attention, universities are robbed of their greatest possibilities when absorbed by a plethora of enterprises that could be undertaken elsewhere.

This conception of the university, as the unencumbered home of disinterested research, requires a second major change. It is clear that as industrial society's appetite for knowledge has increased, there has been indiscriminate addition to the burdens borne by universities instead of creating new institutions to meet new needs. If the university is to divest itself of its organizational excess baggage, it will be necessary to create a large number of entirely new institutions, capable of mobilizing a wide variety of natural scientists, social scientists, and technicians whose work will be mission oriented. Thus, there would be centers for research in urban systems, independent institutes for applied research in the natural and social sciences, and so forth. These would resemble in some ways present organizations like the Brookings Institution or the RAND Corporation, but would have far greater diversity in purpose and personnel. There could also be the development of organizations devoted to the fusion of social research and social action, to tackle some of the social problems with which universities have been tinkering in the name of community service. "Think tanks" unrelated to universities could have an independence and flexibility they could not enjoy in the necessarily more confining atmosphere of universities.

It can be argued that creating new research centers unrelated to universities is unsound intellectually, and constitutes a retreat from a conception of the university that has been remarkably successful. Some would argue that the experience of specialized institutes in the past has been that they lost their intellectual vitality when cut off from the variety and scope of disciplines represented in a university. But this has not been the case outside the United States, and the transformation of institutes in the United States into universities may have been caused more by financial imperatives than by fear of intellectual sterility. In Western Europe and the Soviet Union, the institute pattern has not appeared to cause a breakdown in research creativity.

Beyond the matter of new institutions, there is the need to encourage and protect scholarship by increasing the scholarly activity of learned societies. Far too many of the constituent societies of the ACLS have become little more than placement agencies for members. Few have provided intellectual leadership in their disciplines, and they have for the most part been silent through the recent *Sturm und Drang* of the higher learning in America. These proposed shifts are suggestive rather than prescriptive, but recent experience has clearly shown that some modification of our current conception of universities is imperative.

It is also true that the rapid growth of American universities and their penetration by industry and special interests have tended to change not only the environment in which scholars work, but the very definition of scholarship itself. We have tended to assume, perhaps more in America than in Europe, that the definition of a scholar is elastic and may be stretched beyond its historically limited meaning to include "knowledge workers." In recent years the definition of the "intellectuals," "knowledge workers," and "scholars" has not been clear because the environments which formerly separated them have become increasingly similar, particularly with respect to their scale, work styles, and organization. It would be useful to distinguish between knowledge workers associated with large-scale organizations which are mainly concerned with the *application* of knowledge to current problems, and scholars who are mainly concerned with extending the boundaries of basic knowledge with little concern for its practical ramifications. By this standard, even many persons holding academic appointments would not be scholars. In America there has always been resistance to the view that knowledge, irrespective of subject, is intrinsically valuable. The dominant tendency has been to accord value to knowledge insofar as it is *useful* in social, economic, or political enterprises. For this reason an argument that scholars must reject the demands for their work to be "relevant," is likely to strike many in the academic community as sentimental antiquarianism. I insist, however, that by

37

simply changing masters, the local community action agency for the Department of Defense, is to betray the fundamental mission of the scholar. Scholarship must have no master other than truth, scholars no "social imperatives" other than the disinterested and unfettered pursuit of knowledge. The university and the scholar cannot be true to their basic mission and at the same time cater to the ever shifting demands of students, government, industry, and community groups. This does not mean, of course, that scholars must divest themselves of the obligations of citizenship. The scholar as *citizen* may devote some of his energies to political or social causes, but this must not be confused with the current demand that scholars become political partisans, or mere experts who provide intellectual ammunition to politicians contending for power. If free scholarship is to survive this century, we must now begin the slow and painful process of liberating universities and scholars from ideologies and political entanglements which compromise research and destroy the trust essential to the free pursuit of truth.

CAN SCHOLARSHIP BE MADE LESS CULTURE-BOUND?

Wm. Theodore de Bary

The simple answer to this question is "Yes," if by "culture-bound" you mean that the scholar is always subject to certain limitations of his cultural horizon, which can be overcome to some extent by exposure to other cultures. But scholarship, as distinct from the scholar, is above all a discipline. It forces the would-be scholar to check himself, to recognize the limitations of his knowledge and experience, and to submit his cultural prejudices to reexamination in the light of new evidence. Viewed in these terms the question is far from simple. How can scholarship as a discipline be criticized as "culture-bound?" Isn't it precisely the means by which we overcome our cultural and parochial limitations?

From this latter standpoint one might say that in principle scholarship, as the West knows it, is universal in scope, whatever its limitations in a particular instance as practiced by a given scholar. The drive for universality itself is what has compelled us to develop self-conscious, self-restraining scholarly disciplines, which are themselves the products of culture. While we consider it desirable that scholarship should not be culture-bound, and that it should continue to strive for universality, we recognize that this aim can be achieved only by accepting certain "bounds" or "limits" in regard to proper methodology. We could never hope to be totally unbound, to be "culture-free," as it were, for that methodology must be developed within some culture. The price of cultural self-transcendence is greater cultural self-discipline.

In another sense, however, considered in relation to the major cultural traditions, scholarship is neither universal nor inevitable. Not all cultures have developed scholarly traditions, or at least anything recognizably like ours. Among the major Oriental traditions it was China that most exalted scholarship, personified in the mandarin who was a "scholar-official." The ruling elite were supposed to have scholarly—cultural—qualifications of a humanistic sort, and the dominant Confucian tradition stressed intellectual values. Japan too shared in the Chinese scholarly tradition but was never wholly committed to it. Indian and Islamic civilizations had their own forms of scholarly endeavor, reflecting their own social, cultural, and religious experience, but noticeably different from the Chinese in many respects.

Along with these differences among individual cultures, East and West, the rough generalization can perhaps be made that scholarship in the West has tended to be extensive and extrovert in its development, while the characteristic disciplines of the East have tended to be more intensive and introvert. The significance of this distinction derives from a general difference in the pattern of their social and cultural development. Much could be said on the point; oversimplifying, perhaps, I would suggest that in Western cultures centering around the Mediterranean this "extensive or extrovert" character was generated in part from Greek science and the dynamic of the Semitic religions, while it is lacking in those cultures east of the Khyber Pass that were little influenced, if at all, by these expansive forces.

One result of this is that Western scholarship has been committed to the idea of public discourse. Its disciplines acknowledge the need to test one's views or conclusions in the open court of scholarly debate, to submit them to public scrutiny and challenge. It exposes itself to contrary evidence and argument, and above all deliberately opens itself to new experience. Of course, something of this type of argument can also be found in the great Oriental civilizations—in the Upanishadic discourses, the dialogues' of the Buddhist scriptures, the conversations of the Confucians, the "public cases" of the Zen masters, and so on. But most of that argument in the Orient has been pursued in the opposite direction. Rather than working outward to establish universality through the processes of publicly verified sciences, they have tended to stress the universality of inward experience. They have tried to show the inherent limits of argument and empirical evidence, to point to something beyond words and concepts, something deep within. For them the deeper the experience the closer one came to the common heart of things.

Thus it was that Western scholarship, as expansive as Western explorers and as outgoing as Western missionaries, discovered the classical traditions of Oriental scholarship, instead of the latter reaching out to discover the West. Thus also, but more slowly to be sure, Western education has reached out to include Oriental civilizations within the scope of liberal and humane learning. In principle our education has been committed to the same goal of universality as our scholarship, though in practice it may have often—if indeed it has not always—fallen short of that goal. Just as practice never fully measures up to the ideal, education always lags behind scholarship. Most supposedly educated people in the West are unaware of the achievements of Western scholarship in studying other cultures. Relatively speaking, however, both Western education and Western scholarship—with, to be sure, more abundant resources to draw upon—have gone further in studying Asian cultures than the Asians have in studying each other. The West had to do this, in fulfillment of its very nature. The East did not feel the same need. It worked inward, not outward, and was simply there to be discovered.

Where both Western scholarship and education have been most "bound" or limited has been in the very process of extending themselves. In attempting to enlarge their experience of the outside world, they have sometimes neglected the traditional sources of their own strength, and having become the models for modern Asia, have contributed to the neglect by Asians of their own cultural and spiritual roots. The result has been identity crises all over the place, East and West.

One cannot become less culture-bound by total repudiation of one's own culture. Radical rejection of one's past has the effect of effacing one's identity and cutting off the sources of one's strength. The Japanese's remarkable capacity for adaptation and assimilation of others' cultures derives from their equally remarkable capacity to stay in touch with the past, to continue the active exercise of so many traditional disciplines in the midst of great social and cultural change. The more revolutionary approach of the modern Chinese has brought less change, less openness, less transcendence of their traditional limits. Successive revolutionary movements in the twentieth century, each more radical than the one before, have only compounded China's alienation from its own past. The result, paradoxically, has not been to open up China to the West but to produce almost total isolation from the world.

There has been another sense however in which Western scholarship and education have been "bound" or limited in the very process of extending themselves. In reaching out for new knowledge the West has felt the need to structure it and work out its interrelations. Its scholarship has built up a massive accumulation of knowledge and an imposing edifice of learning. Why then are not more young people today impressed by this "house of intellect?" Why do so many look upon it, on the contrary, with mistrust or hostility? Indeed there are those who look upon the West's passion to structure knowledge as rendering it unsuited to experiencing or appreciating what has been most valued in the Oriental traditions. Western scholarship is accused of imposing its own concepts and structures upon new bodies of data or experience, and of distorting them in its own image.

Such distortions of our perception or arbitrariness of interpretation unquestionably occur. But can they truly be laid at the door of Western scholarship? I am still open to persuasion on the point. So far, however, I see the fault as lying with certain preconceptions of some Westerners rather than as inherent in Western scholarly methodology. How does the acceptance of scholarly discipline contribute to these misconceptions? Are not the limitations involved more individual, temporal, or local than methodological? From my own experience I would say that it is the disciplined scholar and student who is best able to penetrate and appreciate what other cultures have to offer. In my teaching I have found that those undergraduates come to the deepest understanding of the Oriental humanities who have already achieved some mastery of the Western humanities. This is because the mastery involved is more truly a mastery of themselves than of the material.

Oriental peoples do have different ways of looking at things, of experiencing them. And these modes of perception may well become the subject of either personal experience or scholarly study for the Westerner. But insofar as the scholarly study is concerned, what is there in the basic methodology of Western scholarship which handicaps the new enterprise? On the contrary I would see as creative and fruitful the interaction between Western scholarship and science on the one hand and the cultural or social experience of Oriental peoples. The full significance of each becomes clear only in the light of the other. Thus I am aware, in modern times, of Orientals' bringing important new insights to Western arts and sciences, but I am not aware of their developing essentially new and different forms of scholarship.

The real problem in our times, it seems to me, is not that we are culture-bound but that we are culture-burdened. It is precisely in the vast expansion of our horizons, in our incorporation of so much new knowledge into the house of intellect, that we have over-reached ourselves. By this I mean our "selves." The house of intellect is today so imposing, so awesome, that the individual self is simply overpowered by it. The greater our success in adding to the already mountainous accumulation of scholarly literature, the more forbidding seems the student's task in mastering it. Faced with such a challenge, the likely reaction is one of hostility and rejection. Rejection not necessarily of all of its parts but of the whole establishment of learning which is inescapably involved in the production of scholarship.

The interests of young people reflect both the resistance to or reaction against this cultural burden and the desire to discover new forms of experience which may help them to endure the pressures and tensions of cultural and social change. In almost all countries where there is the freedom to express it, we see the urge, especially among the young, to share in the range and diversity of possible human experience, made present to everyone today by the exposure to world cultures. There is a taste for the exotic, a search for the strange and bizarre, a quickness to imitate or appropriate everything foreign in preference to anything familiar. It reflects, on the one hand, the emptiness and sterility of much of everyday life in the modern West, and on the other an appreciation of human possibilities that have previously been ignored. If the Beats found Zen, the Beatles discovered the sitar, and Allen Ginsberg urges "transcendental meditation," it is only a belated recognition of values whch might have been—and by some were—recognized long before. There are, too, deep incongruities in the process. Among Japanese youth, the radical activist or the go-go fan of American rock-and-roll, neither of whom would ever sit still for *zazen* (that is, "sitting in meditation"), is bemused by the eager young Americans who come to "sit" in the monasteries of Kyoto and Kamakura. The avant-garde American poet who writes from a Zen hermitage in Japan contrasts with the serious Buddhist scholar and thinker who, unable to get much of a hearing in his own country, looks to America as the promised land for Buddhism. Similarly with the generally cynical attitude of Westernized Indian intellectuals toward the Western infatuation with Indian swamis, or the ambitious young Chinese scientist, who has never paid much attention to Confucius and Lao Tzu, and is surprised to find that some Americans do.

Thus the attractions may vary, and may even appear to be contradictory or to cancel each other. Still, beneath the shifting fashions of contemporary exotica is the feeling that one can no longer accept his own culture until he has tested it against others', nor can he accept limitations on his own experience or self-development which have only parochial sanction. And this process of self-negation which young people have been going through, of denying one's own culture while delighting in others', cannot but have an effect on education.

Before considering the implications for education,

49

however, we must take into account another marked characteristic of these trends among world youth. At the same time that they open themselves up to new experience, their quest is often for some principle of integration or discipline, some means of managing within themselves not only the overwhelming plenitude of possible new experiences but the enormous burden of past culture and modern technology our society carries with it. Thus the youth who appears to reject all traditional restraints at home is often the most dauntless and indefatigable in taking on the rigid disciplines of Zen or radical activism. The appeal of Che or of Maoism, too, contrasts with the appetite for new cultures by its deliberate stripping down of the individual for revolutionary action. It gives a new sense of self-mastery to the man who finds the weight of established institutions and inherited culture too oppressive. It enables him to assert his naked moral will against all the intellectual complexities of modern life.

Mao Tse-tung, of course, has his own reasons and his own compulsions for taking such a stance. In the depths of his puritanical peasant soul he cannot tolerate concessions to the realities of modern life, which demand so much intellectual attention and therefore intellectual freedom. Nor can he accept compromises with the experience of others which would tend to undermine ideological authority and revolutionary discipline. Hence his condemnation of so-called "bourgeois revisionism," which to him stands for selfish individualism and laxity in matters of principle. In a society that has never known a real bourgeoisie, this is an anomaly that betrays Mao's unconscious acceptance of a traditional moralistic standpoint (somewhat distorted), as opposed to the freer ways of the West. That this new version of an old puritanism should attract the "liberated youth" of the West is another anomaly, but not so strange if we consider that Mao's hostility to Western bourgeois culture corresponds to their own feelings of alienation, while his puritanism plays on their sense of guilt.

For China itself Maoism represents both a rejection of the bourgeois West and a traditional anti-foreignism, essentially defensive and reactionary, shielding the Chinese people from new influences and new options. It cannot in the long run succeed. Withdrawal and isolation from the world, even the Communist world, will not solve Mao's problem, and neither will it solve ours. His isolation is largely born of failure—not only the immediate failures of the Great Leap Forward and the communes, but the prolonged difficulty China has experienced in adjusting to a world of which China is not the center, as Chinese have traditionally assumed. Our own isolation by contrast has been born of apparent success. We have indeed been at the center and forefront of the world, leaders of a triumphant civilization which until now has faced no serious challenge. Only recently have we had to question whether our basic values were universal. There has been steady progress built upon unquestioned assumptions and undaunted faith. Our educational institutions have evolved almost effortlessly from medieval roots in the Christian community and the classical tradition. Never have we endured the almost total shock experienced by the other great world civilizations when their cultures were largely uprooted by the storm of advancing Western civilization and their traditional forms of education were abruptly terminated in favor of some recent import from Oxford, Berlin, or Teachers College. Mao Tse-tung is the offspring of this devastating assault on his mother culture, and if we cannot appreciate the depths of resentment and cultural shock which have produced his unreasoning intransigence, it is partly because we have never experienced anything like it in our own history.

We shall, however, experience it in the years ahead. How violent the process is depends on how well we understand it, how well we can distinguish what is valid and healthy in the criticisms to which our culture and society will be subjected, and how much of the attack must be resisted as negative and unconstructive.

In one form or another we shall have to submit to the same searching critique, the same self-negation, which these other civilizations have passed through. But we can derive some benefit, if we will, from observing the symptoms of maladjustment, of alienation from traditional society, of protest against the establishment during the past century of so-called "modernization" in Asia. Above all, we must be sympathetic to the search of these people for something of human value which can bridge the chasm between the rejected past and the rootless present. For Mao—to take again the extreme but nonetheless typical case—will never be emancipated from the past until he has greater insight into it and becomes reconciled to it, until he reopens Chinese history and civilization for examination and becomes aware of what ghosts from the past still haunt him, even at the pinnacle of his power and authority.

As education builds upon the past and prepares for the future, we must, in the process of reconciling ourselves to one another, reject nothing from each other's past that may help us to understand both our strengths and our hidden weaknesses. It should be a process, moreover, through which Asia can make important contributions to a new world culture and a new humanism. In this way we shall be helping not only ourselves but Asians as well. They shall gain the place in the world culture to which they are entitled and the self-respect without which they cannot become full participants in a new world order.

This development must be seen as a process of growth if it is to fulfill its true mission. For each people it must be rooted in their own cultural soil and grow organically from it. In American education, as I have said elsewhere, it will involve first a basic grounding in Western civilization. "It is not that Western civilization should always have priority, but it must for us. We are

Americans and start from there, or we make a false start." [1] Having done this we can then move on to discover other civilizations and other liberal arts, becoming at the same time more self-critical about our own.

For scholarship the same holds true. We cannot become less culture-bound by abandoning our own culture, but only by seeing that our study of other cultures fully satisfies the highest demands of Western scholarship. In their truest light these standards are self-critical and the best means for overcoming our own cultural biases. Only that kind of scholarly discipline can help us to become less culture-bound.

1   W. T. de Bary, "Education for a World Community," *Liberal Education*, Vol. L, No. 4 (December, 1964), p. 15.

LEARNED SOCIETY OR PROFESSIONAL ASSOCIATION?

George Winchester Stone, Jr.

THE QUESTION, "Learned Society or Professional Association?" is to be considered in the larger context of another implied question about the status and function of the "Learned Society in Today's Democracy." Both questions are pertinent, and they seemed to shake up a group of active reformers at the last general meeting of the MLA. The spokesman of the group, Mr. Louis Kampf, rather scored the MLA for its seeming antiquarian interests and ineffective otherworldliness. Wrote he "Thousands stay away from the annual meeting because they find it trivial or boring, and other thousands have never joined the MLA because they find it irrelevant to their *intellectual* and *professional* concerns. The staff should try to understand the times into which we are moving. . . . The structure allows hardly more than 150 people to participate meaningfully in planning its activities." Quite a series of accusations! The MLA now has 26,000 members, and if Mr. Kampf's assumptions are correct, the throbbing activity and active interests of a mighty mass of scholars are controlled by, and not well served by, seven-tenths of one percent of the membership, and therefore the Association is not widely democratic.

That his facts are not correct, and that his energy for reform is exceeded only by his lack of awareness of what the MLA is, and does, and has done for the past ten years is not much to the point of this discussion, and will be dropped save for the kernel of an idea he has presented—his condemnation of a learned society as irrelevant to the intellectual and professional concerns of its membership. The revolt which, in a long and most active business meeting last December, catapulted him into the second vice-presidency over a German scholar of some standing gives a kind of real-world piquancy to discussions of any learned society. "Surprising things happen," writes Mr. Kampf, "when important issues are discussed openly—and all of us must learn to live with the possibility of such surprises."

Under the cry for intellectual and professional interests, what the reformers seemed really to mean was intellectual commitment to wiping out current political and social ills, and not to professional interests of the members, or to the intellectual probing into and aesthetic evaluation of the literary heritage of the Judeo-Christian-Classical world with which most of the members work in some ten modern languages. Hence the tenor of their resolutions concerning the war in Vietnam, resistance to the draft, boycotting of government agencies, developing black studies on college campuses, preserving freedom of speech and action for the Eldridge Cleavers of the world, problems of the inner city, and alleviating poverty in the ghettos. All of these items certainly have to do with the larger aspect of the topic of our conference, as it relates to political democracy in the broadest sense.

Professor Sidney Hook, however, in his major address the evening before at the MLA meeting (conspicuously unattended by the reformers) had pointed out that these problems are the concern of all of us as citizens, but perhaps should not dominate every aspect of our waking moments: they are our concerns as citizens in community action, at the ballot box, in dollar backing or supportive effort in municipal, county, state, and national campaigns. The function of a "learned society," however, lies in its threefold operation as discoverer, preserver, and disseminator of knowledge—whatever knowledge, that is, which it takes for its province—music, or art, or literature, or Biblical exegesis, or history, or philosophy, or geography. And herein, of course, the specializations that have come about with the explosion of knowledge in our time are important as functions of the division of labor which alone can make social gigantism work for the benefit of all.

I think the distinction between the larger concerns pertinent to all of us as citizens and grown-ups—concern with political and social ills, national priorities and the like—and our just as legitimate scholarly and professional concerns with our chosen subjects is important. Having made this distinction I turn to the narrower topic "learned society or professional association?"

The recent history of the MLA, for example, parallels that of many another large and growing learned society. It reflects the way of the world, as Mr. Irving Rouse's presidential address to the American Anthropological Association this past year indicates.

As to the balance between learned and professional activities which must prevail, I believe, in a modern association, let me review for a moment what has happened within the MLA as it has quietly changed and adjusted, and led its members without the fanfare of activist reform so fashionable today. I chart these happenings as inevitable and healthy, and I constantly illustrate all my remarks by allusion to the MLA, the Society which I know best.

When I attended my first MLA meeting in 1930 I was impressed by two facts: (1) that several hundred scholars would travel long distances at Christmas to listen to one another's papers on specialized topics, arguing furiously about the contents and presentation; and (2) that some of these papers and many others thoughtfully prepared got printed four times a year in a chubby learned journal, rather forbidding in appearance. The articles, however, having passed through the fire-baptism of professional and scholarly editorial scrutiny and evaluation, often seemed to be revisitable and to offer something to the waters of the spirit year after year after year.

These two activities constituted for me the image of the MLA, and when I read the address of Professor Nitze, given the year before at Cleveland, I learned something else, namely, that this group of top-notch scholars was defining the activities of a learned society as "single-minded devotion to research." The scholar-teacher as a functionary in the United States was taken for granted. Beyond that—pedagogy, per se, and professional concerns were for others, and were certainly not central concerns of our learned society in the 1930s.

This stance, of course, represented a rigid, and I may say a narrowing concept of scholarship, not at all present in the edicts of the founding fathers of the MLA in 1883. And the term "research" lacked in 1929 the fascination, the universal approval, and the eminent prestige that it enjoys today—when business has seen profit, industry has seen livelihood, and government has seen survival in the activity the word is supposed to denote in the various fields of science. Yet it seemed then to be

61

the new thing, the breakthrough for commitment, the cutting edge for the future.

The MLA then was run by an Executive Secretary, a Treasurer, several committees, and one clerk fresh out of high school. Eleven hundred members attended that 1930 meeting, and we felt, even then, that bigness was upon us. Some sighed for elbow room, and talked of selectivity. Total membership was 4,055. Dues were $3.00, and the books published by the MLA about that time were *Problems in Shakespearean Penmanship* (Tannenbaum); *Writings Ascribed to Richard Rolle* (Allen); *The Consecutive Subjunctive in Old English* (Morgan Calloway). Yet it looked to some as though the rarified atmosphere of scholarly "research" might be diluted by the numbers gradually gathering around the MLA standard.

Now from six to nine thousand are present at annual meetings; dues are $15.00 and going up. The Executive Secretary works with a staff of sixty, in quarters that cost $100,000 in annual rent. He operates with twenty standing committees who call upon the skilled, professional, and scholarly services of over 1000 members. The administrative staff divides the labor of preparing a variety of publications besides *PMLA*, which has doubled its issues, of organizing and running the foreign language program, of preparing for annual and regional meetings and many, many conferences, of housing important clearing houses of information in the modern language fields, as well as the Center for Editions of American

Authors. The large staff has, through the concern of several Executive Secretaries, been provided with the necessary fringe benefits of a pension plan, hospitalization, job security, and promotional advancement. Unionizing will probably not come to the staff, for their needs are suitably cared for. But professionalism to a high degree has been provided in this basic area of "learned society support."

The largest volumes of publication in the last decade seem to some members to have wandered rather far afield from those scholarly productions which characterized the MLA in the thirties. And in the 1960s the learned society has carried the weight of its name and the momentum of its activity into fields of pedagogy, government, artistic creation, and international humanistic concerns which could not have been conceived in the 1940s or even the 1950s. The course of MLA's expansion undoubtedly parallels that of other large societies in the ACLS group.

But let me be specific. Knowledge of foreign speech is basic to the reading of foreign literatures and critically evaluating and interpreting their styles and sensitive reactions to human concerns. The MLA, upon the assumption that few people of the United States had a knowledge of foreign languages in a world becoming more and more internationally interlocked, took upon itself in 1952 the task of revitalizing the whole method of teaching modern languages. In 1961 it published with funds from a huge Government contract a volume of twenty-eight surveys and studies in the FL Program. Fourteen of these contained statistics concerning foreign language enrollments in public elementary schools, secondary schools, and colleges. Only such fact-finding surveys could reveal the strength or weakness in the teaching of foreign languages on a nation-wide basis. They raised important questions as to the holding power of the teaching that was going on, and provided information absolutely necessary if the society were to seek funds to move into the second stages of pedagogical activity, which in turn would ultimately affect the humanistic scholarship with which future members would be concerned.

The other fourteen reports consisted of various fascinating field studies. One was an account of the needs in ten cities for people who could speak foreign languages. The reports revealed the need for intelligent speakers of foreign languages in law courts, in social welfare agencies, in police systems, in libraries, and in telephone companies. This very study itself alerted responsible city officials to their deficiencies in the numbers of foreign language speakers available to them, and to career opportunities for those who would bring to their jobs a speaking ability in a foreign tongue. A second study surveyed foreign language teaching on television. A third and fourth gave descriptive evaluation of programs for teaching foreign languages in public elementary and secondary schools, respectively, in five geographical areas across the United States. In these reports, please note, the profession was helping itself, and the members were widening their professional responsibilities. They were not relying upon professional educators from the Office of Education to prescribe methodology. Newness of approach and fullness of participation were the keys. A fifth report was a 400-page study of the needs for improved and increased teaching of the neglected languages. A sixth produced a valuable (and since updated) annotated bibliography of cultural readings in the six common languages. A seventh provided a depth study of the academic, professional, in-service training of modern foreign language teachers in a single state, Connecticut. Another reported on the interrelationship of second language learning and English. Another report gave practical advice for solving the rising problem of adjusting college courses to take into account the inflow of students well trained and nearly fluent in foreign languages, and of in-service training for graduate assistants and beginning instructors. And so the reports went —all having to do with aspects of the profession far removed from the individual research concerns of university professors.

For a number of years before this, the MLA produced teachers' guides for beginning French, German, and Spanish in the grades. And along the way it broke the pattern and stranglehold of publishers in beginning language text books for college with a new type called *Modern Spanish,* which treats language not as accumulated vocabulary threaded on morphological paradigms, but as spoken dialogue with pattern practice, and with audio accompaniments. Since testing is a function of teaching, the MLA wound up a half-million dollar government contract to produce teacher proficiency tests in five languages. Of late the MLA has begun a new professional organization of Modern Foreign Language Teachers which embraces the basic interests of those teaching languages, as opposed to groups segregated by specific languages. And it has provided for them a separate professional journal.

The spill-over of these aspects of the study of teaching foreign languages to English has been enormous. It started in 1959 with a year-long series of conferences which produced the influential pamphlet *Basic Issues in the Teaching of English;* this led to the formation of the Commission on English (outside the MLA), which led to summer institutes funded by the U.S. Office of Education, paralleling in a way those concerned with the teaching of foreign languages, to improve the range, practice, and potential of the teaching of English in the secondary schools. Among its publications the MLA has provided the institutes with materials, and has organized in the colleges and universities the Association of Departments of English, which is gradually now involving department chairmen throughout the country in the integrated problems of improving the profession. In these activities the MLA has cooperated fully with the National Council of Teachers of English.

Nine times in its long history the MLA has revised

its Constitution to reflect broadening intellectual interests and professional responsibilities of its members. Its basic document now defines the purposes of the Association: "to promote study, criticism, and research in modern languages, and their literatures, and to further the common interests of teachers of these subjects."

All this we feel is to the good. The learned society in such a basic subject as modern languages and literatures accepts its responsibility for professionalism, and the pedagogical steps which lead to it. The question to be asked is whether in doing so have we confused our objectives in our spread of general tolerance and widespread activity. What has become of our concern for the traditional aspects of higher learning, and criticism and literary research? Are scholarly, pedagogical, and professional concerns as interrelated as we have thought?

Seven years ago in pondering this issue I reread Lessing's *Laokoon,* and my old teacher Irving Babbit's *New Laokoon,* on the confusion of the arts. Being an eighteenth-century type I wondered for a moment, whether a *New New Laokoon* might not be indicated, with a shift of subject from the confusion of painting and poetry, to an apparent confusion of scholarship, pedagogy, and professionalism. "Painting and poetry," wrote Lessing, "should be like two just and friendly neighbors, neither of whom indeed is allowed to take unseemly liberties in the heart of the other's domain, but who exercise mutual forebearance on the borders, and effect a peaceful settlement for all the petty encroach-

67

ments which circumstances may compel either to make in haste on the rights of the other."

I concluded at the time, and am still of the opinion, that no *New New Laokoon* is called for to delimit and keep separate these three fields precisely because they are so interrelated. But I must reserve time in a moment to readdress myself to the important question of the division of labor, the limits and the ground rules which qualify a learned and professional Association to perform its basic function in our total society. And in this I will have to pour a libation to Roman Terminus, the god of boundaries. For the MLA, though it has moved along professional and pedagogical lines "to further the common interests of teachers of modern languages," has not issued edicts as to teaching loads, or class sizes, or salary scales, or policies as to sabbatical leaves, or tenure—the AAUP is concerned about some of these issues, the NCTE about others. And this division of labor seems sound, for tenure affects not modern language teachers alone, nor does a sabbatical policy, nor a teaching load policy, nor a salary scale. In these fields colleges and universities, because of variance in size, clientele, and endowment, have obvious responsibilities. But the MLA has issued policy statements concerning the teaching of foreign languages and English, fields in which its members have particular competence.

But a word about the other side of the balance between learned society and professional society. The MLA, with all of the activities to which I have referred and many more of late in the professionalizing of its order, has not only maintained, but has added to its concern for the "learned aspects" of its purposes.

Since learned journals are important in effecting these purposes, the MLA in 1957 sponsored two conferences of forty editors of learned journals in our field to discuss common problems of editing. The conferences resulted in the *Handbook for Editors of Learned Journals* (1959). The MLA also published three series of "Facts of Journal Publishing" at three- or four-year intervals from 1955 through 1963. *PMLA* published in 1957 "American Journals in the Humanities: A Guide to Scope and Editorial Policy," which lists the editorial policy statements of forty-eight journals in the field as a help to scholars for placing their articles.

As for *PMLA* itself, it widened the scope of its annual bibliography from a national one to an international one, which now lists over 4000 items published throughout the world in the field of modern languages and literature during the previous year. For the past ten years it also has carried on with the new *Shakespeare Variorum*.

Recognizing the increasing importance of linguistics, the MLA started and fostered the beginnings of the Center for Applied Linguistics with its focus on the problem of English as a second language. For ENSCO it produced a critical and annotated bibliography of "Great Literature, East and West."

As to book publication, the MLA involved about

three dozen scholars in four "Reviews of Research and Criticism." With the university presses strengthened, the MLA ceased book publication and started a book club, which distributes to scholars at a discount the annual surpluses of the university presses.

As for scholarly aides, the *MLA Style Sheet* has been revised several times and is used by 109 journals and over 40 presses. Significantly, the MLA has published "Approaches to Literary Scholarship," by Professors Fredson Bowers, William G. Moulton, Robert E. Spiller, and Northrup Frye. This work defines for prospective graduate students the fields of textual editing, linguistics, historical criticism, and philosophical and aesthetic criticism. To alert authors about publishing contracts, the Association, under the editorship of Oscar Cargill, published *The Author and His Publisher*.

In 1962 the MLA absorbed the work of the Index Society with its program for bibliographical and indexing projects in our field. In 1963, it established the Center for Editions of American Authors, now funded by the National Endowment for the Humanities.

The MLA has, moreover, taken a prominent part in international congresses in cooperation with the International Federation for Modern Languages and Literatures (FILLM). The Executive Secretary has sat with a committee of the ACLS, the Council of Library Resources, and the American Historical Association in order to plan in an orderly fashion (both in this country and abroad) for photocopying of foreign scholarly documents.

In response to the trend in our land toward scholarly interest in contemporary literature, the Council created a new category of membership, Honorary Fellow. The list is impressive: Jorge Louis Borges, Rene Char, Friedrich Durrenmatt, Romulo Gallegos, Jorge Guillen, Aldous Huxley, Robert Lowell, Archibald MacLeish, André Malraux, Francois Mauriac, Marianne Moore, Pablo Neruda, St. Jean Perse, John Crowe Ransom, Jean-Paul Sartre, Ignazio Silone, Guiseppe Ungaretti, Thornton Wilder, and before their deaths, T. S. Eliot, Albert Camus, William Carlos Williams, and Ernest Hemingway.

The keynote to the MLA activity in the past decade is balanced expansion and the acceptance of professional *and* learned responsibilities. All moves, furthermore, have involved conferences of scholars averaging about 200 per year. The scholarly and humanistic philosophy permeating them has reflected the principles followed by the Executive Secretary in every conference. (These principles are spelled out, for foreign languages, in the Report of U.S.O.E. Conference, 20 May 1960; for English, in *Issues, Problems, and Approaches*, 1961.)

The MLA Program Committee has for ten years at the General Annual Meeting sought to remind the members that they live in a wider context of life than that defined by their particular scholarly specialties. It

71

has, therefore, had its annual address given by lawyers, politicians, scientists, classical scholars, poets, philosophers, and statesmen. But standing at the very center of the MLA, along with its productions on foreign languages and its stimulus to a new look at English teaching, is the publication of fifty scholarly books in all modern language fields, a distinguished and readable learned journal, and the twelve activities outlined above, aimed to support and expand literary scholarship in this country.

A final question. What are the limits of expansion of this or any learned society? I return to the basic issue of all time and all civilizations, namely, that of the proper division of labor, and the essential but *separate* functions of man as a citizen in a democracy, and as a member of a learned society. I hope, earnestly, that the two, each valuable in its own right, and each practicable without interference, will be kept separate. Expansion within the bounds of a compassable and useful definition is sound, but expansion beyond those bounds may mark a step toward the return to anarchy and chaos.

I have respect for what Newman called the "wild living intellect of man," and its pounding desire to shift and change, involve itself in all sorts of things, but I also have a fondness for the old Roman deity introduced by Numa, who persuaded his subjects that the limits of their lands were under the immediate care and superintendence of Heaven. The divinity was the god Terminus, with a temple on the Tarpeian Rock, who presided over boundaries. He was, as you know, represented with a human head, without feet or arms, to intimate that he never moved after he was established. So firm was the belief in boundaries that when Tarquin the Proud wished to build a temple even to Jupiter himself on the Tarpeian Rock, the god Terminus alone refused to give way. I invoke this deity now, not as a bulwark for "the establishment," but as a sensible reminder that universities and learned societies have unique functions within a democratic system, functions defined by their purposes, and useful to democratic society as they fulfill those unique functions—the discovery, preservation, and dissemination of knowledge, critically probed, imaginatively communicated, according to the highest professional standards.

The ordering, analysis, and advancement of knowledge, devoid of partisan application, is pertinent to a learned and professional society. Partisan application is an individual privilege and prerogative. We do have, after all, both democrats and republicans, communists and socialists, the orthodox religious, agnostics, and atheists within the MLA, but its common bond relates to none of these persuasions, and the association is the more humanistic as it eschews partisan activity. In his personal life each member has his three- to four-ring circus of activities in which to involve himself. In the MLA *all* are concerned with the compilation of knowledge, its relationships, its history and its permanent and transhifting values.

Unless a learned society seeks increased *professional* achievement it loses significance in the modern world. Unless a learned society recognizes some principle of division of labor necessary to civilization it loses its unique function in a democracy, for which, after all, it has been given privileges, perquisites, and responsibilities.

The MLA has divided the labor of its intellectual concerns within a structure which is elastic enough to meet the genuine interests of its members. In 61 *Groups* and *Sections* at annual meetings it discusses the traditional specialties of the membership, and allows both the young and the seasoned scholars to present ideas and to discuss them. Its four to five *Forums* for discussion of new and untraditional areas (film, science fiction, transformational grammar, etc.) and its 64 *Seminars* for small group discussion on any topic which three or four members wish to throw open for debate (such as autobiography as an art, Sephardic studies, issues in training of young China specialists, Blake's illuminated works, Renaissance symbolism and allegory, contemporary African literature, etc.) allow for a wide range of interests to be satisfied. The follow-up is terrific in its intellectual potential. When the "Renaissance Group" issues a 164 page bibliography on topics needing research, the "Literature and Society Group" issues a select bibliography of 49 books and 158 articles for consideration, including one by Mr. Kampf called "The Scandal of Literary Scholarship." The boundaries are there, but the fields enclosed within them are wide.

It may be correct and practical for a learned society such as the American Political Science Association, or the American Sociological Association to caucus and take a stand on short-term political and social activities, and to involve the members *as an association* in the aftermath of Watts, Newark, and Vietnam—though I do not think so. Individually, according to one's conscience, yes! As an Association, no! The Association must work according to the long-term scholarly analysis and synthesis which looks toward permanent solutions to the problems that vex mankind. As to the organizational involvement in establishing national priorities for human effort and budgetary support—no! Block support, however, by a large number of individual letters to individual congressmen for the National Endowment for the Humanities may, of course, be effective, and may help preserve for a while humanistic activity as a living facet of worth in a world bent largely toward other values. Such activity on an individual basis lies within bounds as it is individual and provides means to discover, perpetuate, and communicate the joyous, the rugged, the hard and the beautiful in those fields of the arts and humanistic sciences for which the ACLS stands.

Dr. Johnson concludes in his *Rasselas:* "In life there is little to be enjoyed: much to be endured." The illumination which good scholarship gives in literature, music, art and history increases the enjoyment and mitigates the endurance factor—tough as it may be.

I wish to study, preserve, and communicate learning in these fields, and crave a society of scholars with high professional and pedagogical standards with which to associate. This area is but one of many in life, but it is worth the attention of the dedicated few, who also as citizens concern themselves with other complications of a democratic way of life.

LEARNING AND THE PROBLEM OF UNDERGRADUATE EDUCATION

William J. Bouwsma

IT IS A curious fact, and one closely related to the concern of this paper, that the immediate reaction of a university scholar who is invited today to express general views about education is likely to be anxiety. Not only will an opportunity of this kind probably be a considerable novelty in his life, but the subject is also almost certain to strike him as outside his "field"; herein, of course, lies much food for thought. Hence, in what will also be in various other respects a rather personal statement, I feel some need to begin by presenting my credentials for discussing the issues suggested by my title, and to describe something of the perspective that has shaped my contribution to this discussion.

Since my remarks may lend themselves to a different interpretation, I should like too to emphasize their conservative inspiration. I have been an academic historian for two decades, and after an interval of some years I am about to return fully, and with sensations of gratitude and relief, to teaching and scholarship. I hope, therefore, that what I have to say will not be interpreted as an attack on scholars or on learning. Furthermore, I have been moderately active in a number of learned societies. I have been president of one small and rather specialized society, and for some years on the council of another. So I hope that what I have to say will not be construed as an attack on learned societies. And if I am somewhat critical of the present relations of scholars and learned societies with undergraduate education, I am myself implicated in any charges I may bring against them.

But a university career, perhaps especially in the remarkable circumstances we face today, can take unlikely turns; and for the past two years I have been serving as academic vice chancellor at Berkeley. In this role I have had some experience with assessing and trying to meet the demands of faculty and students, appeasing angry alumni and other members of the outraged public, developing plausible explanations of improbable events and complex decisions to lay Regents, informing and placating legislators and other public officials, and mediating among these various and often incompatible groups. It is primarily these responsibilities that have stimulated the impressions and very tentative conclusions I want to present here, though I should also make clear my belief that the problems that will concern me in this paper now, in varying degrees, beset all universities, and perhaps not only in the United States. Although I shall refer to developments in California, this is not intended as another in the long and tedious series of reports about the latest events at Berkeley.

My conclusions will be tentative for various reasons, among them the fact that I too am by preference a rather specialized scholar who is unaccustomed to the subject at hand. In addition, academic administration, however stimulating, hardly provides now an ideal situation in other respects for systematic reflection about education. Although they are often called on to exert "educational leadership," university presidents, chancellors, and even vice chancellors are becoming increasingly further removed from the educational process itself; they are rarely able, if only for lack of time, to make useful statements about education, though they may often be heard to speak, a bit wistfully, of doing so some day, possibly after retirement. This is obvious, especially to the men who run universities, and I make the point chiefly to explain why what follows may be long on observation but relatively short on prescription. The point may also hint at the peculiar advantages, opportunities, and responsibilities of learned societies, a subject to which I will return.

This conference itself testifies to our general concern about the present plight of universities, and as representatives of scholarship we are rather specifically troubled because in our society universities have become the major patrons of learning. I can offer no reassurance about our predicament; indeed, I believe that we are in far more serious trouble than most of us have yet realized. Higher education, it seems to me, is experiencing a crisis of the most fundamental and dangerous kind—a crisis of public confidence that involves all elements in our diverse constituencies and threatens private and public universities alike. In spite of the conviction of scholars that learning in its various forms has never been more important and more urgently required in the modern world, in spite of the ease with which we can all demonstrate this and the frequency with which it is asserted, universities have never been so unpopular or under such broad attack.

Let me emphasize that criticism of us comes from every direction, some of it from places where we would least have expected it. Thus even our best students often insist that we are "irrelevant"; and if they frequently seem vague about the meaning of the word, this only suggests that it express discontents almost too deep and general for articulation. We all know how many students stick to their academic tasks grudgingly or with an uneasy sense of copping out, because they can think of nothing better to do, or because the alternative may be Viet Nam; many others drop out altogether. Even in the graduate schools a high proportion of students, admitted with the best possible credentials, give the impression of being still chiefly unsatisfied seekers; and they too, disappointed once again, often simply disappear. Under these conditions I suspect that we would be unwise to count on our students' eventually thinking better of us as alumni and thus helping to improve the unfavorable balance of opinion about us among older groups. Meanwhile our present alumni increasingly baffle us by their general apathy to our glowing accounts of the triumphs of scholarship and their skepticism or indifference when we describe imaginative new courses and promising educational reforms. Minority groups and the poor are angry with us because we do so little for them, although it is often unclear what they seek from us that is legitimately ours to bestow. And men in public office, or eager to attain it, have discovered that few gestures are more popular with the electorate than an attack on higher education.

There are doubtless various reasons why this is so, but I think we would be dangerously wrong to attribute fundamental importance to public indignation over campus disorder and political militancy, and to count on a restoration of public confidence with a change in the political climate. The reaction against campus radicalism by a profoundly frightened society is closely related to the basic problem, and it has also focussed attention on higher education and accelerated a more general kind of public discontent, which might otherwise have developed more gradually. But even more serious forces have been at work, and to get at these I should like to stress the remarkable unanimity of our various critics. In their distrust and disapproval of us, if on little else, old and young, politicians and students, Right and Left, are in basic agreement. Not enough has yet been made, I think, of this fact and of the strange alliances it has produced. The real problem stems from the general assumption of our public that the primary task of the university is the education of the young who are entrusted to us as undergraduates, and the widespread and growing conviction that we are presently failing badly with this essential responsibility. And I am inclined to believe not only that this indictment is largely valid, but also that the cause of our failure lies in an unhealthy relationship, the product of several decades of development, between learning and education, especially undergraduate education, in the university. This is the deeper lesson to which the apparently "political" criticism of higher education should direct our attention. And, if I am right about this, learned societies indeed have particular cause for concern.

A speech by Governor Ronald Reagan to the Commonwealth Club of San Francisco on June 13, 1969, supplies an unusually useful illustration of this analysis. Much of the Governor's talk was in defense of police tactics (i.e., the use of shotguns and gas) against Berkeley demonstrators during the altercation over the People's Park the previous month, and this part of his speech was received, predictably enough, with applause, and two standing ovations. But Reagan went on from here to present a remarkable explanation of Berkeley's endemic political troubles. They were the natural expression, he suggested, of "the disappointment and resentment of an entire college generation—a generation that is justifiably resentful of being fed into a knowledge factory with no regard to their individuality, aspirations or their dreams." Although the voice was the voice of Ronald Reagan, the words were remarkably those of the Free Speech Movement, which would thus appear to have made a notable convert. And the Governor went on to offer himself as an ally of discontented students. "The challenge to us," he declared, "is to establish contact with these frustrated young people and join in finding answers before they fall to the mob by default."

He did not identify very clearly the questions to which he sought answers; and in view of his suspicions about the influence of professors on the young, his own "answers" seemed somewhat inappropriate, and in any case hardly adequate to the greatness of the challenge. His crucial point, nevertheless, seemed to be that professors should spend more time with their students. He said that teachers should be persuaded to teach, and it was evident that he believed they are not presently doing so. To this end he proposed that research should be subordinated to teaching and that it should cease to be the primary standard by which a university measures its quality. He also suggested that professors might work harder (in context this evidently meant that they might do more teaching) if they did not have tenure. He clearly wanted education to be restored to the university from which he believed it had largely disappeared, and he also called on education itself to become relevant. His conception of relevance was made explicit in his conclusion: "The few subversives on our campuses will be much easier to handle if the so-called silent majority has inner convictions, beliefs, and confidence in our society and in us as adults."

The Governor's depressingly familiar notion that the political problems of the campus are caused by a "few subversives" and his belief that they can be solved by properly "handling" these troublemakers should not, however, mislead us about the seriousness of what he was otherwise saying. And I think we should take the most careful note of his views partly because of their surprising coincidence with those of the SDS and the Radical Student Union. They are shared by many others; men in the center as well as at the political extremes also aspire to a better world where the young can once again rely on a body of stable values and ideals, and there is widespread agreement that the central task of higher education, without which all else is in vain, is precisely the development in young people of inner convictions, beliefs, and confidence in the justice of our

86

social order. The reaction of his San Francisco audience to the Governor's reflections about education was as enthusiastic as to his defense of the police. According to one reporter, "It was at this point that the audience . . . rose for the third time to give Reagan an ovation." [1] Nor are other illustrations of the point difficult to find. During May, for example, in a similar transition from concern over disruptions on the campus to larger questions about its function, 27 members of the California state assembly voted to hold up *any* appropriation for the university and state college systems until they "give some answers" about where higher education is going; and this angry group of legislators was finally defeated by a margin of only eight votes. Indeed, only professors appear reasonably satisfied with the present state of affairs in the university, though even they show signs of increasing anxiety and restiveness in the face of mounting, though still generally mysterious, public disapproval. How could things have gone so wrong?

If I am right about the radical character of current discontent with higher education, it would obviously be a mistake to diagnose the problem as simply one of communication, to be solved by larger Offices of Public Information and glossier announcements about Nobel prizes, foundation grants, and technological discoveries that promise vast economic benefits. We have, I suspect, rather seriously misjudged our public and its concerns, possibly out of a somewhat presumptuous judgment of

1 *San Francisco Chronicle* (June 14, 1969).

our own about its "interests." It may be that the public has been less materialistic than we have assumed, that it is actually far more concerned with the values of the young than with the development of a mechanical fruit-picker or even the discovery of a new element. This, at any rate, is the essential message I pick up from our present critics; and accordingly I believe that their discontent should be taken with the greatest seriousness, and for deeper and more respectable reasons than our own material dependence on them.

I would argue, indeed, that however crude the form of the criticism to which we are being subjected, it makes a point with which even those of us whose interests are well served by the present focus of the university are in at least partial agreement, and which has obscurely troubled our consciences. For it reflects a serious conception of education, one that is rather different from what most of us now represent as academic men but one that happens nevertheless to be the traditional view of education, as opposed to mere training, in Western society. This is, of course, the idea of education as *paideia*, as the transmission of the deepest insights, attitudes, and values of a society, the most precious legacy it can pass on to succeeding generations. Education, in this conception, should convey a society's general beliefs about the meaning and purpose of life, its perceptions about the coherence of experience, its concern with social duty and the relation between the needs of life in society and the development of the individual personality. This is what education has consistently meant for those men in the past who have thought most deeply, and with the steadiest and most pervasive influence, about education. This is what education meant to the Greeks and to the pedagogical theorists of the Renaissance and the Enlightenment, and it survived in the classical curricula and the denominational colleges of the last century. (I do not mean to idealize these last in all respects, but at least they had a sense of purpose, a *paideia* to communicate.) And much of our present crisis is a consequence of the persistence into our own time, if only half consciously, of the idea of *paideia* as the model governing our sense of what education ought to be, while at the same time it has been largely disappearing from our universities. Higher education is now under judgment by this standard, and it has been found utterly and profoundly wanting.

Let us take a brief look at ourselves with the idea of *paideia* in mind. As we all know, today's university has been largely shaped by what Jencks and Riesman have called "the academic revolution," i.e., in their own words, "the rise to power of the academic profession." This development has been understandably satisfying to the profession itself, and it has also been useful for meeting many of the specialized needs of modern society. It is admirably suited to the training of specialists and the preparation of various sorts of professional men. But it happens also be very badly adapted to the needs of undergraduate education, which has been persistently regarded—except perhaps in the university itself—as our primary obligation. It is very little concerned with the transmission of values, except for such values (I do not minimize them) as may be inherent in or necessary to specialized training; with general ideals, except indirectly and incidentally; or with the meaning of human experience and the purpose of life, even as questions requiring perennial discussion. It is thus about as indifferent to education as *paideia*, unless there is a specific *paideia* of scholarship itself, as one can possibly imagine.

Above all the academic revolution, though made possible by the increasing practical importance of some academic groups to society, has resulted paradoxically in a peculiar kind of detachment from society. The academic profession, strong in the sense of its new importance, has come to regard the university as largely its own possession, as an essentially autonomous entity with a moral obligation to resist the pressures and demands of the society that brought it into existence, although this obligation is of course generally rationalized as somehow in the ultimate interest of society itself. The professor has come to see his natural community not as the local society from which his university draws its support but rather as the national or international community of scholars, and the university itself as the agency through which that larger community operates. Within the university the academic profession therefore insists (with general success) on the right of the faculty to make decisions about courses and curricula, in accordance with its professional interests, somewhat in the manner of a priesthood, the keepers of mysteries too sacred to be treated by the multitudes. It has been almost equally successful in asserting the right of the faculty to select other faculty, and so its priorities are effectively perpetuated. And it has also sought the right to determine who should be admitted as students, with the frequent result in practice—highly satisfactory for our disciplines but less obviously sound from the standpoint of society as a whole—that we devote most of our attention and our resources to the best students: i.e., to precisely those students who would appear to need them least. Finally, the academic revolution has been largely responsible for our emphasis on research even in our teaching; although I reject the ease with which the distinction between research and teaching is often made, it is nevertheless true that they are often coordinated chiefly by converting the classroom into an opportunity for reporting research. Again I should emphasize that these developments have produced important benefits and met important needs. I want only to point out that these needs have been served at a heavy cost: namely, the sacrifice of education as *paideia*.

For what the academic revolution has meant is, in effect, the triumph of learning over education, the laissez-faire pursuit of the specialized interests of learned men over the general formation of the young. Absorbed in the search for truth, we have given a minimum of attention to the coherence of the entire intellectual enterprise of the university, to problems of meaning and value, and to our deeper social role. Seeing knowledge as an end in itself, we have lost sight of its broader human purpose; and professors have tended increasingly to operate on the assumption that education consisted essentially in the scholar's training his successors. In this light the university may well appear as the last strong-hold of nineteenth-century liberalism, and in this respect not the most advanced but the most inert of institutions. It has operated on the vague assumption that if each scholar does his thing, all will somehow work out mys-teriously for the best; through random exposure students will somehow emerge as educated men, and society should be content. The assumption has turned out to be dreadfully wrong.

At the same time I do not want to convert these remarks into just another attack on higher education. It is characteristically American to blame the schools when things go wrong, out of an apparently unshakable con-fidence, one of our more awkward legacies from the Enlightenment, that education can cure all ills. Univer-sities are therefore likely to serve as a convenient scape-goat in time of crisis; this is the negative corollary of the importance we ourselves have attributed to them. The problem of the modern university cannot, however, be dealt with so simply; the failure of universities to educate is only a symptom of deeper difficulties. For universities, however we should prefer them, are not divinely set apart from the rest of our society, in a position to act on it and to solve its problems, so to speak, from the outside. They are rather, however remotely, agents of society and bearers of its assumptions, and they are therefore hardly capable of supplying by themselves what has been lacking in our culture as a whole. I am inclined, therefore, to take the attack on higher education as a sign of profound discontent with the general quality of modern life. If the universities now produce so much anger because they appear to lack a coherent educational ideal and a clear sense of purpose, one has only to look at the world that has produced them to discover the true cause: a world that is itself fragmented, specialized, mechanistic, incoherent, and lacking in clear and generally accepted values. By the same token, if this kind of world now provokes widespread discontent, we may be in the presence of a far deeper set of cultural changes than we have yet supposed.

Under these conditions, I must confess that most proposals for university reform seem to me remarkable chiefly for their superficiality, and even when most likely to prove effective, calculated rather to intensify the educational problem than to solve it. Little can be expected, as I have suggested, from university administrators. Even if they were not too busy fending off political militants on one side and the outraged public on the other, or trying to mediate among the numerous special interests that each demand a piece of the multiversity, they are virtually powerless in the realm of

educational policy, too suspect among both individual-
istic faculty and angry students to exert significant influence on the educational process. But even under the
most favorable conditions I am not persuaded that administrators really know what to do. Their common
receptiveness to innovation and experiment in undergraduate education (and I hasten to add that I do not
exclude myself from this indictment) strikes me less as
a virtue than as a confession of educational bankruptcy,
and more likely to subvert the tasks the university presently performs well than to benefit students. The faculty,
meanwhile, has a vested interest in a status quo which has
worked so well from its standpoint; and most administrators have found professors, on the whole, depressingly reluctant to abandon their disciplinary commitments in order to engage in novel pedagogical schemes
that seem to them, with some reason, of doubtful promise. The only innovations that appear to have much
attraction for professors are those calculated to improve
teaching in their own subjects, for example freshman
seminars that introduce students at the earliest possible
moment to the problems and the spirit of modern scholarship. I think it important to observe that most faculty
members are, in my experience, intensely serious about
their teaching and very good at it; the point is that their
goals as teachers are largely disciplinary goals.

Nor do I see much reason to flatter students for
their insights into what is needed in the way of educational reform, though I think we should take their

discontents very seriously indeed. Student proposals for educational change seem to me no less timid and confused than those coming from other sources. This is in part, I think, because of a contradiction between the need for coherence, meaning, and value, which seems to me the real significance of the demand for a "relevant" education and which points in one direction, and the natural desire of the young, which points in the opposite direction, for more freedom and even fewer prescriptions than are now to be found in most undergraduate curricula. In addition the constraints of an unsatisfactory education have encouraged students to believe that the problem lies in constraint itself and thus that its solution lies in greater freedom. In any event, student proposals for change have either seemed trivial or tended to reinforce existing weaknesses, for example the elimination of grades, the abolition of language requirements, or the introduction of courses dealing with contemporary problems, courses that would merely add another set of specialized inquiries to our already disjointed instructional program. The educational proposals of students give the impression rather of shifting about on a bed of pain than of a movement toward health; and I find the most significant hints of the needs of students not in their curricular suggestions but in such phenomena as their growing interest in the occult, which I interpret as a sign of longing for a kind of meaning and coherence they have been seeking vainly in more respectable quarters. The alleged radicalism of students makes many of our fellow citizens uneasy; I would suggest, on the contrary, that students, like the rest of us, have not been in a true sense nearly radical enough about education, the values it should serve, and the ways it could be made to serve them. On the other hand, I have never quite understood why we should expect, as some of my colleagues appear to expect, greater wisdom about education from the youngest members of the academic community than from the rest of it. There are, however, many romantic assumptions about that deserve closer scrutiny.

Another conception of relevance has also been frequently proposed, from outside as well as inside the university, as the principle for desirable changes in higher education: that the university should focus far more of its attention on immediate social problems and needs. This may well be desirable and even necessary in some cases, but it should be clear that it has to do primarily with the role of the university in the training of specialists; it offers no solution to the problems of undergraduate education, which it would compound rather than ameliorate. For it should be obvious that this kind of educational relevance merely opens the way to an even higher degree of conformity than at present to the practical requirements of a fragmented and aimless society; I think, therefore, that it would only deepen our common discontent. Furthermore I suspect that excessive adaptation to present needs would in the long run prove selfdefeating and likely rather to hinder than to facilitate

96

the accomplishment of those specialized and practical missions in which we are effective. At no time in history, perhaps, have men seen more clearly that things are changing rapidly, that yesterday's problems are no longer today's, and that tomorrow's problems are therefore likely to be different from those we now face. If the university is to retain its general usefulness, as I hope it can, it must not constantly transform itself to solve particular and passing problems. Far from making the university truly relevant, this would only insure its irrelevance for the future.

If my analysis of the problem of the university is valid, we would thus appear to be in a fearful dilemma: we crave a true *paideia* as the heart of the undergraduate curriculum, yet the quality of our culture, whatever the discontents that may be gathering, seems to exclude it. And if the problem is ultimately cultural rather than educational, there would seem to be little that we could do to attack it. Yet, even though at the outset of these remarks I promised little in the way of remedy, I am not altogether without hope. For if I noted the valuelessness and incoherence of contemporary culture, I emphasized also the gathering of a movement in the opposite direction, a movement, it may be added, of the kind that has usually become already irresistible by the time it attracts general notice. And I see a few signs that the conservatism of the academic profession (its own revolution accomplished) and our general blindness to the nature of the dissatisfaction with higher education that now surrounds us may be giving way in one of those mysterious, uncalculated cultural adjustments that even universities cannot permanently resist.

Thus I would point to the emergence at Berkeley of several new undergraduate programs which appear on first inspection utterly different but on a deeper level reveal, it seems to me, common characteristics that may be of considerable significance. The oldest and most highly developed of these is Professor Joseph Tussman's lower division college, recently described in his book *Experiment at Berkeley* (New York: Oxford University Press, 1969); the second is a new residential program in modern history and literature within the College of Letters and Science; the third is a program, or more precisely a series of programs, dealing with the historical experience, the culture, and the present predicament of minority groups: Afro-American studies, Mexican-American studies, Asian-American studies, and American Indian (or native American) studies.

Since the first two have had difficulty in obtaining faculty support and the third is only now being developed, I can hardly make any large claims yet for the success of these programs, and they certainly do not demonstrate that Berkeley is about to change its basic character. Nevertheless they are alike in several interesting respects, and in their similarities I suspect that there may lurk some hint of the more general adaptation required of us. All three are undergraduate programs, conceived outside the traditional departments, interdisciplinary in structure, which aspire to make use of the learning available through the established disciplines for educational goals that have been formulated with relative clarity. Professor Tussman is concerned to deepen a student's values and his understanding of himself in relation to society by examining the ethical and social thought of other periods of historical crisis; the program in history and literature aims to help students "locate" themselves in relation to their own culture (and might be described as a WASP identity study); the aim of ethnic studies is to deepen our understanding of minority groups and perhaps also (for students from minority backgrounds) the individual's sense of relationship to his community. In pursuit of these goals, furthermore, all three programs are far more highly organized and prescriptive than most other undergraduate curricula. All three are also evidently concerned with values, and based quite directly on a conviction of their central importance for undergraduate education. And finally, in each case, this primary concern is expressed through a study of the experiences, the collective wisdom, attitudes and insights, and the tradition of some community, whether the larger cultural community of the West or the particular community of a ghettoized ethnic group.

But this, I submit, is very close to the general meaning of *paideia;* and in the emergence of these and other similar programs (I have no doubt that they are now also appearing in many universities) we may perhaps discover an important lesson for the times. One of our difficulties would appear to be not so much that our society is lacking in *paideia*, but that it is peculiarly pluralistic. What is therefore missing is chiefly consensus about the content of *paideia*, and the solution to our problem may well lie in the frank recognition of diversity, in a clear perception that our society is characterized by a number of *paideiai* each of which may be appropriate to explore, in the interest of a genuine undergraduate education that will provide students with some sense that they inhabit a universe of serious values and dependable relationships. Indeed, each of the *paideiai* among us may need exploration in the interest of an ultimate social unity, since an awareness of differences must come before we can recognize what we have in common.

I know that there are dangerous possibilities in what I am proposing, even if the danger may be somewhat reduced by the acceptance of this pluralism. *Any* coherent educational program, organized around shared traditions and values, that aims to transmit to the next generation the attitudes we cherish most deeply will inevitably suggest indoctrination and myth-making, an imposed conformity of mind, ethnic and cultural self-centeredness. I must also admit that I sometimes doubt whether the liberal, pluralistic, intellectual universe that I would choose to transmit to my own children, for all its limitations, is fully consistent with the kind of *paideia* that our society seems increasingly to require. But unless we acknowledge the intensity of the need for it

and set to work ourselves, as academic men, to satisfy
it in ways consistent with the abiding values of the university, I am afraid that others will aspire to satisfy it,
and in ways that few of us would care for. And I am
also afraid that the time is growing short.

And this is where learned societies might, if they
chose, play a constructive role of the greatest importance for learning itself, for education, and for their
continuing and fruitful interaction. As for learning, I
think the societies might begin to prepare for a time
when the universities may be less hospitable to some
kinds of scholarship than they have been in the past.
Should this occur, it would be important to have some
alternate location for learning, a location not vulnerable
to the charge that scholarship is merely an esoteric spe-
cies of self-indulgence carried on at the expense of
education. The scholarly accomplishments of the seventeenth and eighteenth centuries may suggest that we
need not despair at this prospect.

But learned societies might also do something for
education and in the process help considerably to insure their own future in our society. They could accept
a major responsibility for meeting the educational needs
of our time; recognize that although learning may be
an end in itself under some conditions, it should serve
an ancillary role for most undergraduates; and help the
universities to devise new programs, organized around
the ideal of *paideia*, in which the substantive results of
the scholarly disciplines are deliberately subordinated

to the methods and values inherent in various forms of intellectual inquiry.

More concretely, I think that the learned societies might establish standing committees to consider what the several disciplines could contribute, individually and collectively, to an undergraduate education that is primarily concerned with problems of meaning, value, and the general goals of our society, and then employ their considerable influence among scholars to convert the intellectual resources now confined to the separate disciplines to genuinely educational ends. I should like, for example, to see historians shift some of their attention from questions directly about the past to an inquiry into the general value of the historical consciousness itself, its difference from other ways of viewing the world, and how it might be communicated to students as the true goal of an education in history rather than as just an incidental benefit that can be left to take care of itself. I should like to see anthropologists describe more consciously and aggressively the contribution anthropology could make to every student's intellectual formation, and then build courses around this as a primary goal. I should like to see philosophers, literary scholars, musicologists, art historians, sociologists, and the whole range of disciplinary specialists represented in the university all engaging in similar enterprises. And then I should like to see them collaborate on the more general problem of coordinating their various educational resources for the development of a curriculum that would leave students not only with the sense that learning has some general meaning for their lives but also that their education has indeed been the transmission of *paideia*. If I have made little reference to the natural sciences in this connection, the reason is partly that they have already taken important steps toward defining a broader role for themselves in the undergraduate curriculum, while the humanistic disciplines affiliated in the American Council of Learned Societies, which seem especially needed in such an enterprise, have so far been strangely passive.

This conference is, however, a hopeful sign that their passivity may be approaching its end, and this is a good omen for education. For I continue to believe that humanistic learning, however derelict it has recently shown itself, can still serve as a vehicle for *paideia*. Nothing else, at any rate, can be depended on to transmit to successive younger generations such threatened virtues as openness, flexibility, tolerance, rigor with oneself, a feeling for the complexity of moral and social experience, and finally humility, which are basic to the ideal of civility so eloquently described by Professor Sutherland.

EDUCATIONAL STRUCTURES
AND CULTURAL
FRAGMENTATION

Christopher Lasch

FACED WITH A student rebellion that scorns the university and often scorns reason itself, university professors prepare to defend the university as the last surviving citadel of "civilized values," without perceiving that it is precisely the university's failure to defend those values, together with the general inhumanity of advanced industrial society, that has produced the student revolt as a reaction. It is not merely that the university has promoted research in counterrevolution and technological destruction; that it encroaches, an overgrown real-

estate corporation, on its neighbors; that much contemporary scholarship serves to legitimate oppressive
institutions or to justify bankrupt policies; or that the
curriculum ignores the most urgent needs of the times.
These failures reflect a deeper crisis in Western culture,
one that cannot be understood if we confine our attention to its more obvious symptoms.

Unfortunately the student movement itself—not
surprisingly, considering the scarcity of reliable advisors
among professors—has for the most part done just that:
it has concerned itself with the superficial manifestations
of cultural crisis and has raised questions about the university in a form that enables professors to evade the
underlying implications of those questions. To mount
a convincing counterattack against demands for "relevance" that are often crude and openly anti-intellectual
does not greatly tax the professorial mind. If relevance
is demanded in the name of contemporaneity or joined
to demands that higher learning become an active agency
of social and political change, it is not difficult to formulate an appropriate reply:

> If we demand this kind of relevance, what becomes
> of the Chaucer scholar, the philosopher who is in-
> terested not in justice but in sense perception, the
> art historian investigating the origins of the Gothic
> cathedral? It would be an act of barbarism, not a
> way of advancing our civilized purposes, to aban-
> don these activities or to intimidate these scholars.

. . . We cannot allow the total politicization of the universities. . . .[1]

There the argument all too often rests, with both parties unconvinced and sullenly hostile. Such arguments can end only in blows: disruptions, acts of revolutionary defiance, reprisals and counter-reprisals—in short, the "total politicization of the universities."

The only way out is to formulate the question of relevance more precisely than before and to understand why it should have become an overriding issue at this particular time. In asking for a better understanding of the cultural issues that underlie the crisis of higher education, I do not mean that we need a "better under-

---

1 Marshall Cohen, in a symposium on "The Future of the Humanities," *Daedalus* (Summer 1969), p. 732. The poverty of most discussions of higher learning now taking place is suggested by the inability of those who demand "relevance" (to what?) to articulate a reasoned rebuttal of this position. Instead they lapse into rhapsodic praise of "the kids," who are said to know more than their teachers. "Literally, increasingly, they have more *experience*. Every day now I encounter students who have seen more of the world than I have seen. Some of them have hitched across the country in the wake of Ginsberg and Kerouac, and others have made their way up and down the coasts of Africa. They have wept beside the Ganges and spent the winter in Khatmandu. . . . Compared to those of us who have garnered our most recent experience from our bibliographies, they simply *know* more." (Herbert Blau, "Relevance: The Shadow of a Magnitude," *ibid.*, pp. 667-8). This attitude effectively absolves the teacher of any responsibility to furnish advice and leadership to his students—most of whom are desperately seeking it, in spite of the impression created by a self-righteous few. If the students know more than we do, how can we pretend to teach them anything?

standing of today's students." Attempts to trace the current unrest to the "generation gap" are an elaborate evasion, whether they are used to condemn student protest or to exalt it. Even if it were possible to generalize about a whole generation of students, and even if there were any truth to the competing views—that the present generation, as its admirers claim, is endowed with an ineffable wisdom peculiar to itself, or to the contrary that young people permissively raised in affluence resent all authority and prefer the simple solution of violence to reasoned discourse—theories of generational conflict would still be inadequate to explain what is wrong with the university or what might be done to reform whatever is wrong. The present generation of students is not alone in insisting that higher education has become largely irrelevant to the search for truth. The same charge has been made, in one form or another, by almost every critic of higher education writing in recent years. It has been evident for a long time, as a middle-aged professor of philosophy put it in 1964, that

> many of our more distinguished exemplars of the academic life today are not exactly men for whom wisdom and truth mean more than money, honor, and reputation. . . . These are the things that really spur the young academic hopeful to toil endlessly in laboratory or library, grinding out his research, picking up Guggenheim and Rockefeller grants as he ascends the ladder of success, and finally turning

110

out to be an international authority on hormone solutions or the pottery of the Zuni Indians. And as for wisdom and truth, these are not the things that matter academically.[2]

This indictment of the university was familiar long before the student rebellion of the sixties took shape. But even if we were to concede that generational conflict has added a new dimension to the controversy over higher education, we should still have to explain why that conflict tends to focus on "irrelevance" and not on some other set of issues. The question can be answered only by a critical analysis of the contemporary university, the educational system of which it is the pinnacle, and the culture which the university and the school system as a whole are designed to perpetuate.

The modern system of education is the product of several centuries of historical evolution, of developments that have affected all advanced countries in varying degrees but in roughly the same way. Three things in particular stand out as having shaped the present system: the modern state's administrative need for uniformity, the peculiar requirements of an economy rationalized along capitalist lines, and more recently the demands of twentieth-century technology. At the same time the educational system in advanced countries has retained a lingering commitment (though hardly more than a

2   Henry B. Veatch, *Rational Man* (Bloomington, Ind., 1964), p. 62.

verbal commitment) to an ideal of knowledge that ante-dates and transcends the requirements of advanced capitalism—the conception of knowledge as a means to justice, goodness, and wisdom. This ideal (which is not to be confused with the more recent view that knowl-edge is an end in itself) has not always been associated with formal institutions of learning. Until the end of the eighteenth century the schools performed quite specific functions, such as training professionals. It was only in the nineteenth century that they began to claim a monopoly of culture in the broadest sense. Indeed the tendency of the school to absorb all other means of cultural production was one of the consequences of industrial capitalism and political centralization in the realm of education. Another consequence was a redefini-tion of knowledge that drew a sharp distinction between objective, instrumental knowledge—which in the nine-teenth century began to be reserved for science—and the subjective "inner truth" associated with poetry. I shall attempt to show that the school's monopolization of culture was closely related to the fragmentation of knowledge—in other words, that the two developments were part of a larger process that has been referred to as the industrialization of culture.

Until the nineteenth century, large sections of the population escaped formal schooling altogether. This fact has usually been taken to mean that the masses lived in darkness and that the eventual achievement of uni-versal education came about because the masses learned to demand it as their birthright. Recent studies, however, suggest that formal education was imposed on the masses by middle-class reformers who saw the school essentially as an instrument of social control—the "civilizing" effects of education being closely associated, in their minds, with the need to discipline people whom the dislocations of early capitalism threatened to render unruly and rebellious. The coming of universal education did not liberate the masses, it merely subjected them to bureaucratic custody.

At the same time it either destroyed or degraded apprenticeship and other informal institutions of learning. Originally apprenticeship had been a broad and variegated institution; nor was it confined to the manual trades, as it is today.[3] Among the laboring classes apprenticeship was often a means, not merely of transmitting skills, but of providing elementary instruction in reading and arithmetic, in conduct and deportment, and in other pursuits necessary for the assumption of adult responsibilities. The upper classes had their own form of apprenticeship, such as foreign travel or sending their children to live with other families. Indeed the "putting-out" of children was a universal custom in the premodern Western world; all classes practiced it, and it should be considered as the most prevalent form of apprenticeship in preindustrial society.

3 On apprenticeship and other informal educational arrangements see Philippe Ariès, *Centuries of Childhood* (New York, 1962), pp. 137-336; also Lawrence Stone, *The Crisis of the Aristocracy* (Oxford, 1965), pp. 692-702.

In addition to this domestic apprenticeship and to the more familiar forms of craft apprenticeship that have survived, in debased form, into our own time, informal schools grew up, often in close proximity to the crafts. The most important were the schools run by scribes, which taught writing and arithmetic to girls as well as boys, to adults as well as children, and to people of all social classes. A painting by Holbein depicts such a school in progress, with an inscription on the master's sign that reads: "Whoever you may be, burgesses, artisans, labourers, women or girls, and whatever your needs, he who comes here will be faithfully instructed for a reasonable fee." [4]

All these informal institutions of learning taught subjects that were later incorporated into primary and secondary schools. Similarly many of the activities later associated with higher education originally had no connection with the universities. These remained professional schools until the beginning of the nineteenth century. For a long time they retained the features associated with their ecclesiastical origin: the use of Latin, the classical curriculum, and a notable resistance to innovation. The universities and colleges were much slower than the rest of the educational system to absorb the lay culture that had always coexisted with the ecclesiastical culture which the schools originally had been designed to preserve. In the seventeenth and eighteenth centuries lay culture was revolutionized by new advances in science,

4 Ariès, *Centuries of Childhood*, pp. 298-9.

political theory, philosophy, mathematics, and the arts; but almost every important discovery in these fields took place outside the universities and in many cases in open opposition to the universities. Scientific societies, private patronage, and other informal arrangements supported lay culture in its advanced forms just as apprenticeship, craft schools, and the family supported its more rudimentary forms. The university, in contrast, was still designed primarily for people bound for careers in medicine, law, and theology, while the secondary schools existed chiefly to prepare scholars for the university.[5]

In time, however, the colleges and the universities, like the primary and secondary schools before them, absorbed the lay culture, abandoned narrow professional training, and redefined the ancient ideal of liberal education as a broad training in civility. In the course of the nineteenth century, the concept of the university as a center for disinterested learning and pure science was added to but did not entirely displace liberal education in the classics and other gentlemanly pursuits. Each of these conceptions was superimposed on previous conceptions, with the result that the twentieth-century university represents a variety of discrete functions that have been incorporaed into higher education at different

5 Many other kinds of scholars, however, passed in and out of the grammar schools without taking degrees. Even formal education was far more flexible and informal than it is today. Thus the grammar schools taught people of all ages, some of them preparing for the university and others in transit to something else. Segregation by age was unknown.

times. It continues to provide professional training not only in the traditional professions but in such fields as engineering, agriculture, social work, and nursing, which formerly would have been regarded as vocations rather than professions. The liberal arts have themselves been professionalized, so that the university at once tries to provide a rounded liberal education for undergraduates and to train "professional" scholars at the graduate level. The idea that "research" is the main business of the university has tended to reinforce the growing professionalization of the liberal arts. At the same time the liberal ideal, as redefined in the late eighteenth and early nineteenth centuries, persists side by side with these other ideas of the university. In order for pure research and the new professionalism to win a dominant place in the university, the proponents of "disinterested learning" had to attack and destroy the genteel tradition, which had come increasingly to identify liberal education with upper-class dissipation. They did not win a complete success, however; that would have required not only the destruction of old-fashioned gentility but the separation of the university from the college and the older professional schools—a solution proposed by Veblen in 1918.[6]

The idea of liberal education survived the collapse of the genteel tradition in the early twentieth century, just as it had survived the abandonment of the classical

6 See *The Higher Learning in America* (New York, 1918), *passim*.

116

curriculum in the nineteenth, and it still exerts a power-
ful influence on higher education. Nor has liberal education lost the essentially ornamental character that it
acquired in the nineteenth century, when it came to be
identified with gentility. Much of contemporary education seems clearly designed, not to impart a thirst for
learning or even to train cadres of technical workers,
but to train sophisticated consumers.[7] A recent study by
Ivar Berg shows that academic training often bears little
relation to the skills required by jobs for which academic
training is considered indispensable. Graduates with degrees in the humanities are eagerly sought by corporations and government bureaucracies not so much
because they possess important skills as because the degree presumably identifies them as people of taste and
decorum. The bureaucratization of careers in business
and the civil service has contributed to this outcome by
placing a premium not on raw ability but on a man's
"background," on his marriage, and on his ability to
maintain a certain style of life. That there is no uniform
correlation between higher education and industrial employment is particularly clear in the case of women,
who are being educated in increasing numbers even

---

7 A weakness of contemporary criticism of the university
by radicals is that it sees the university's exclusive function as
that of training technicans and other members of the "new
working class." (See, e.g., Alain Touraine, *Le Mouvement de mai*
[Paris, 1968], chs. 1, 2). This analysis makes it hard to explain the
survival of the liberal arts curriculum, which is still regarded as
the heart of the university by students and faculty alike.

though the number of career opportunities for women has been steadily shrinking. This apparent contradiction can be explained only on the assumption that one of the chief purposes of higher education, especially in the humanities, is to provide training in sophisticated consumerism and in the sophisticated consumption of culture itself.

The humanities are well suited for this ornamental role because they have largely abdicated their claims to interpret the objective world and have increasingly concerned themselves with the description of inner states of feeling. The split between science and the humanities occasions much concern, but it is not clearly understood how it came into being or how actively the humanities conspired in their own demise. The development of rationalism in the state and in the capitalist economy had as its counterpart in the realm of culture a concept of science that equated objectivity with freedom from judgments of value. Nineteenth-century positivism and its twentieth-century offshoot, behaviorism, provided a philosophical rationale for this new and greatly restricted idea of science, which swept every other conception before it because the material gains that followed the emancipation of science from moral and theological fetters promised to liberate man himself from his age-old subservience to nature. Critics of the new social order taking shape in the eighteenth and nineteenth centuries protested against the over-valuation of the physical sciences and pointed out that unless science came to center on man, liberation from nature would prove to be a new form of enslavement to man-made institutions un-amenable to rational control. These critics failed to win a popular following, however, and by the end of the nineteenth century humanism had taken refuge in the humanities and left the social sciences themselves to the mercy of those who wished to recast them in the image of the physical sciences. Social science became mechanistic, deterministic, and "value-free," excluding from its scope traditional questions about the human ends knowledge should serve. Social science, which should have been a means of human liberation, became a technique of social control.

These developments coincided with the structural reorganization of higher learning in the last half of the nineteenth century—the abandonment of the classical curriculum, the introduction of electives, the proliferation of graduate programs, and the increasing emphasis on professionalism and specialization. The new ideal of disinterested "research," superimposed on the older ideal of liberal education, had the effect of shifting the university's center of gravity from the humanities to the physical and social sciences and from undergraduate instruction to graduate programs. It is unfortunate that the change was resisted not by advocates of a broad and unified conception of professional education and of knowledge itself—such as Jefferson had tried to institutionalize at the University of Virginia—but rather by the partisans of sterile gentility on the one hand or of vulgar utilitarianism on the other. In such a contest the advocates of pure science appeared, even to so penetrating a critic of higher education as Veblen, as champions of enlightened progressivism locked in mortal combat with the Philistines. Few if any observers perceived that the defense of pure science itself rested on the material achievements of modern science. No one seems to have pondered the implications of the position staked out by advocates of disinterested research like Daniel Coit Gilman of Johns Hopkins, who defined the purpose of the university as "the acquisition, conservation, refinement and distribution of knowledge" and went on to argue that the university's pursuit of this goal should be subjected to no narrowly utilitarian test.

> If you persist in taking the utilitarian view and ask me what is the good of Mr. Glaisher's determination of the least factors of the missing three out of the first nine million numbers . . . , I shall be forced to say I do not know; and if you press me harder I shall be obliged to express my conviction that nobody knows; and yet I know, and you know, and everybody may know, who will take the pains to inquire that the progress of mathematics underlies and sustains all progress in exact knowledge.

Significantly, Gilman did not leave the argument there; he added that applied mathematics had played an important role in developing steam locomotion, the telegraph, the telephone, photography, and electric lighting. "These wonderful inventions," he pointed out, "are the direct fruit of university studies." [8]

What is ominous about this defense of pure research is the assertion that although scientific "progress" is the purpose of the university, the results of that progress cannot be communicated to the public or even from one department of the university to another, except in the form of "wonderful inventions." The whole controversy over pure and applied research (or between disinterested learning and gentility) presupposed an almost total fragmentation of culture. In the modern world the unity of culture requires, among other things, a broadly educated public, such as existed briefly in the seventeenth and eighteenth centuries, to whom the results of scientific investigation can be communicated and by whom they can be evaluated.[9] By the end of the nineteenth century such a public had of course ceased to exist. To train such a public, one might suppose, would have been precisely the overriding objective of the new universities. Instead the universities abandoned all but the pretense of a general education (now increasingly identified, as noted, with conspicuous consumption) and sought rather to promote specialized research that would

8 Quoted in Frederick Rudolph, *The American College and University* (New York, 1962), p. 273.
9 See Norman Birnbaum, *The Crisis of Industrial Society* (New York, 1969), pp. 107-113.

lead to "scientific progress." The fact that Gilman himself, in the last resort, had to defend science on the grounds of its practical applications showed that it had become impossible to defend science on any other grounds, since it no longer communicated any meaning to a general audience.

Having thus freed itself from educated criticism, science rapidly identified itself with objective and "value-free" research. The physical sciences became the model for the human sciences. Accordingly the latter turned from the study of man in society to the study of man in nature.

> Sociology . . . wanted to be a precise science, and, since its subject matter was man, it sought to put man under scientific wraps in the most exact ways. There was a fervent movement to dissect, classify, tabulate, simplify. . . . The science of man became the science of fatalism, a curious monstrosity: man now reads nature for its laws, but in order to do nothing but continue to read nature! [10]

The decline of sociology as a critical discipline centering on the need to bring society under rational control opened the way to the uncritical empiricism that has come to prevail in the social sciences and finally even in history and philosophy, while the discussion of values

10 Ernest Becker, *The Structure of Evil* (New York, 1968), pp. 91, 61.

now had to be confined to the arts, which were just then surrendering their claim to make statements about objective reality.

The institutional reflection of these cultural changes is the "multiversity," departmentalized, computerized, ruled by administrative bureaucrats and academic entrepeneurs, and harnessed to the requirements of the warfare state. In such an environment, talk of the need for a critical science of man sounds quaintly archaic. It is likely to be rebuked on the grounds that to allow science to be informed by values would give "subjectivity free rein." Did not Bertrand Russell explain that "whatever can be known, can be known by means of science; but things which are legitimately matters of feeling lie outside its province"? Of course it is exactly this split between science and "feelings" that has contributed so much to the social and cultural crisis of the mid-twentieth century, of which the current upheavals in the university are one reflection. Social science having abandoned its critical function, criticism of the obvious madness of modern society itself verges on madness. "Feelings," banished from science, take refuge in styles of political and cultural radicalism that are increasingly attracted to irrationalist perspectives, to a preoccupation with the occult, and to a celebration of primitive tribalism. It does no good to exhort rebellious students to return to reason and to refrain from "politicizing" the university. As long as reason identifies itself with "value-free" scientific objectivity, the necessary criticism of

123

industrial society, which should be built into the social sciences and the humanities but which they have almost wholly neglected, will continue to find its outlet in bizarre forms of latter-day romanticism. Instead of deploring student activism, those who claim to stand for reason should address themselves to the task, so many times deferred, of constructing an integrated science of man on premises explicitly critical of industrial society.

It seems quite clear that this task cannot be accomplished without at the same time changing the institutional structure of higher education. Faculty-student control must be substituted for the overgrown administrative hierarchy. Teaching and scholarship must take precedence over buildings and government grants. The peripheral and extraneous functions of the university should be pruned away—vocational training, remedial work designed to teach what the high schools failed to teach, custody and detention for the young. (Higher education should be open to people of all ages.) These reforms in turn presuppose the reform of the lower schools and of industrial society as a whole—the destruction of the school's monopoly of culture, the abandonment of formal education as a qualification for work (except for the professions and for university teaching itself), the invention of alternate methods of socialization and preparation for adulthood, the revival of apprenticeship in new forms.

124

In the meantime those who wish to humanize the scientific study of man, if they are to survive in the university at all, will have to find means of combining their energies and talents for a collective attack on the cultural crisis. The best instrument might be a new type of learned society—interdisciplinary, militantly nonprofessional, animated by political and social concerns without subscribing to any of the currently fashionable political dogmas—which would combine criticism of existing disciplines (now provided with various degrees of clarity by some of the radical caucuses in the professions) with the search for an interdisciplinary synthesis of the critical knowledge that exists, almost buried under mountains of empirical trivia, in all of the disciplines relating to the study of man. Sheldon Wolin and John Schaar have recently argued that "the great intellectual task of the present is the task of rethinking every aspect of technological civilization"—of examining "what technological civilization has done to our language, literature, art, politics, and work" and of exposing "the historical choices that were made by reference to the putative benefits of science and technology placed in the service of endless growth and power." [11] This is an admirable statement of the problem, but it is not likely that the American university will become the locus of such an inquiry, as they propose it should—certainly not in the near future, perhaps never. It is still less likely that the task will be taken up by

11 *New York Review of Books* (October 9, 1969), p. 6.

the professional organizations, which are almost wholly given over to careerism and to the discussion of papers designed to promote scholarly reputations in the job market. The work of "rethinking every aspect of technological civilization" properly belongs, at this stage in the development (or collapse) of higher education, to a scientific society independent alike of the professional organizations and the university. It is even possible that a society of this kind might become the nucleus of a genuine university. In the meantime the indispensable work of criticism and cultural reconstruction must go forward, and the formal conditions of academic life hardly seem propitious for such an undertaking.